THE AMERICAN Sampler COOKBOOK

Collected by Linda Bauer

Medallion Books Los Angeles

THE AMERICAN SAMPLER COOKBOOK

Copyright © 1986 by Linda Bauer

An original Medallion Books edition
published for the first time anywhere.

First printing, October 1986

Book design by Graphics Two, Burbank
Interior illustrations by Linda Tunney
Cover appliqué by Christy Cowell

Library of Congress Cataloguing-in-Publication Data

Bauer, Linda.
   The American sampler cookbook.

   Includes index.
   1.Cookery, American.   I. Title.
TX715.B349   1986   641.5   86-23606
ISBN 1-55627-025-9

The Medallion name and Medallion logotype
are trademarks of Medallion Books, Inc.

MEDALLION BOOKS, INC.
5455 Wilshire Boulevard, Suite 1700
Los Angeles, California 90036

Printed in the United States of America

DEDICATION

To my parents who care about others and practice giving rather than receiving. To my husband and children for their kindness, help and patience. Thank you for accepting my distraction with grace.

CONTENTS

Dedication . . . . *v*

Foreword . . . . *ix*

Acknowledgments *1*

1 *Appetizers* *2*
(Dips, Hors d'oeuvres, First Courses)

2 *Salads* *18*

3 *Soups and Stews* *38*
(Soups, Chowders, Chilies & Stews)

4 *Side Dishes* *66*
(Vegetables, Potatoes, Grains, Pasta & Beans)

5 *Main Dish Casseroles, Lunch & Supper Entrées* . . *92*
(Casseroles, Soufflés, Savory Pies, Sandwiches)

6 *Meats* *126*
(Beef, Pork, Ham, Lamb & Veal)

7 *Poultry & Seafood* *154*
(Chicken, Cornish Hens, Ducks, Shellfish & Fish)

8 *Breads* *194*
(Yeast Breads, Quick Breads, Pancakes & Crepes)

9 *Cakes & Cookies* *216*

10 *Pies & Desserts* *238*
(Pies, Cheesecakes, Puddings, Sherbet, Flan)

11 *Potpourri* *270*
(Beverages, Sauces, Relishes, Snacks, etc.)

Index by Recipe *282*

Index by Politician *286*

Index by State *292*

FOREWORD

The American Sampler Cookbook began as a dream in May of 1985, and through the cooperative and friendly efforts of the statesmen who lead our country that dream has become a reality. One purpose of this book is to allow the reader to enjoy some of the favorite recipes of our leaders, and to share in this warmly familial area of our national heritage.

The contributions to this collection reflect a love of good cooking from a variety of ethnic backgrounds as well as different types of food indigenous to particular regions of our country.

While you and your family are enjoying these recipes please remember that you are also helping to feed the starving people of the world. My profits from this book go to the American Red Cross Famine Relief Fund.

Thanks to all of the people who so generously donated their treasured recipes . . . and thus contributed so significantly to relieving the hunger of those less fortunate.

—Linda Bauer

ACKNOWLEDGMENTS

Special thanks to Rose McCloskey, Margaret Johnson, Steve Sloan, Representative John Kasich, Senator Howard Metzenbaum and Linda Hayes who share the belief that fighting world hunger is a worthy cause and felt compelled to give of their time and talents. To Nancy Baggett, our coordinating editor, and Kathryn Jensen and Linda Tunney for their hard work and a job well done. To the staff at Medallion, especially Andrew Ettinger; and to all at the American Red Cross for their support. To President Reagan and his First Lady, and Vice President Bush and the members of congress and their families and staffs for their generous contributions to this book.

Chapter 1

Appetizers

Dips

Hors d'oeuvres

First Courses

NIPPY CHEESE STRAWS

Senator **John C. Stennis**—*Mississippi*

2½ cups all-purpose white flour
¾ teaspoon cayenne pepper
½ teaspoon salt
1 pound extra sharp Cheddar cheese, finely grated
2 sticks margarine
2 tablespoons water

Preheat oven to 300 degrees. Sift together dry ingredients 3 times. With large fork blend cheese with flour mixture. Melt margarine, add water, then slowly blend with cheese mixture. Knead dough lightly and divide into 2 parts. Roll each portion out on lightly floured pastry cloth into a rectangle about ⅓-inch thick. Cut into strips ½-inch wide and about 2-¾ inches long. Place on lightly greased cookie sheet. Lower oven temperature to 225 degrees. Bake 1 to 1¼ hours until golden brown. May be frozen.

Makes about 100 cheese straws.

TOSTADA GRANDE DIP

Representative **John T. Myers**—*Indiana*

My wife and I enjoy hot, spicy foods and this recipe is a particular favorite of ours. It was featured in a southwestern newspaper article as "Tex Mex Dip" and has been called Mexican pizza and various other names. It is a real crowd pleaser here on Capitol Hill as well as back home in Indiana.

3 medium-sized ripe avocados
2 tablespoons lemon juice
½ teaspoon salt
¼ teaspoon black pepper
1 cup commercial sour cream
½ cup mayonnaise
⅛ to ¼ ounce package taco seasoning mix
2 10½-ounce cans jalapeño bean dip
1 large bunch green onions including tops, chopped (about 1 cup)
3 medium-sized tomatoes, seeded and chopped (2 cups)
2 3½-ounce cans pitted ripe olives, chopped and drained
8 ounces sharp Cheddar cheese, shredded

To serve:
Large, round tortilla chips

Peel, pit and mash avocados. Add lemon juice, salt and pepper. Combine sour cream, mayonnaise and taco mix in separate bowl.

To assemble: Spread bean dip on plate for first layer. Spread avocado mixture on top for second layer. Spread sour cream mixture on top for third layer. Add chopped onions for fourth layer. Add chopped tomatoes for fifth layer; chopped olives for sixth layer and shredded cheese for top layer. Serve chilled or at room temperature, along with tortilla chips.

Note: For a hotter dip, add a layer of green chilies or mix some chilies with avocado layer.

Makes 16 servings.

GUACAMOLE

Representative **Tom DeLay**—*Texas*

4 **well-ripened avocados, peeled and**
  diced
2 **tomatoes, peeled and diced**
1 **medium-sized onion, very finely**
  chopped
  Salt to taste
  Black pepper to taste
  Garlic salt to taste
  Lemon juice
To serve:
  Tortilla or corn chips

Combine avocados, tomatoes and onion in a bowl. Add salt, pepper and garlic salt. By hand, mash all ingredients together until smooth; do not blend with electric blender or mixer. Lightly sprinkle dip with lemon juice to prevent discoloration. Serve dip along with chips.

BIG BEND BEAN DIP

Representative **Tom DeLay**—*Texas*

>   2 **cups cooked pinto beans**
>   1 **small onion, chopped**
>   2 **tablespoons bacon drippings or**
>   **butter**
>   ⅓ **cup sharp Cheddar cheese, grated**
>   1 **4-ounce can jalapeño peppers,**
>   **drained, seeded and chopped**
>   **Salt to taste**
>   **Black pepper to taste**
>   **To serve:**
>   **Corn chips or tostada shells**

Mash beans until quite smooth, or blend in blender.
Set aside. Sauté onion in bacon drippings or butter
until soft. Add beans and remaining ingredients to
onion and stir over low heat until cheese melts. Serve
warm.

Makes about 3 cups dip.

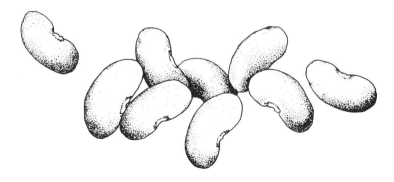

CALIENTE HOT DIP

Senator **Pete Wilson**—*California*
Recipe from: Mrs. Wilson

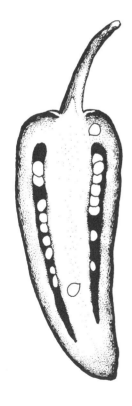

1	16-ounce carton small curd cottage cheese
1	4-ounce can green chilies, drained and chopped
1	large tomato, peeled and diced
3	green onions, including tops, diced
1 to 1½	teaspoons Worcestershire sauce
3	dashes Tabasco sauce

To serve:

      Assorted fresh vegetables or tortilla chips

Mix all dip ingredients. Cover and chill for 3 hours before serving. Serve with cut-up vegetables or tortilla chips.

TEX-MEX CHILI AND CHEESE DIP

Senator **Bob Packwood**—*Oregon*

> 4 15-ounce cans Hormel chili without beans
> 1 pound Velveeta cheese, grated or finely chopped
> ½ to 1 cup chopped onion
> Tabasco sauce to taste
>
> **To serve:**
> Tortilla chips

Combine all ingredients in casserole; stir to blend. Bake in preheated 325-degree oven until heated through. Serve in chafing dish, along with tortilla chips for dipping.

Alternatively, place dip ingredients in crockpot, heat and serve from pot.

SPINACH DIP

Representative **Patrick L. Swindall**—*Georgia*

> 1 **10-ounce package chopped spinach, thawed and well drained**
> 1½ **cups commercial sour cream**
> 1 **cup mayonnaise**
> 1 **8-ounce can water chestnuts, drained and minced**
> 1 **package Knorr's vegetable soup or Lipton spring vegetable soup mix**
> To serve:
> 1 **large round loaf sourdough rye bread**

Combine spinach (uncooked) with all remaining dip ingredients, mixing well. Cover and refrigerate until well chilled.

Hollow out center of sourdough bread and stuff with dip. Break up scooped out portion of loaf into bite-sized pieces to use for dipping or spreading. This dip is also delicious served as a spread for French bread slices or crackers. Or serve dip with assorted cut-up vegetables.

MARYLAND CRAB DIP

Representative **Michael D. Barnes**—*Maryland*
Recipe from: Claudia F. Barnes

        12 ounces cream cheese
         2 tablespoons Worcestershire sauce
         1 tablespoon lemon juice
         2 tablespoons mayonnaise
         1 small onion, minced
           Dash of garlic salt
        ½ bottle of chili sauce
        ½ pound fresh crabmeat
           Chopped fresh parsley for garnish
    To serve:
           Assorted crackers

Blend the first six ingredients together and mound
over a shallow dish. Spread ½ bottle of chili sauce on
top of cream cheese mixture. Arrange crabmeat on
top of chili sauce. Sprinkle with chopped parsley.

Makes 6 to 8 servings.

HOT CRAB DIP

Senator **Paul Trible**—*Virginia*
Recipe from: Rosemary Trible

1½	pounds fresh Virginia crabmeat
3	8-ounce packages cream cheese, softened
1	pint commercial sour cream
1	medium-sized onion, grated
1	teaspoon Worcestershire sauce
½	teaspoon ground (hot) red pepper
½	teaspoon ground oregano
	Salt to taste
	Black pepper to taste

To serve:

Melba toast rounds

Gently break crab into chunks and set aside.

Mash cream cheese with a fork. Work remaining dip ingredients into cream cheese. Heat mixture in double boiler over simmering water until blended and soft. Gently stir in crabmeat. Transfer to chafing dish. Serve with melba toast.

Makes 20 to 25 buffet servings.

HOT CRAB HORS D'OEUVRES

Representative **Thomas S. Foley**—*Washington*

When entertaining at home, my wife, Heather, and I enjoy preparing the following dish for guests.

1 **stick butter or margarine, softened**
1 **5-ounce jar Kraft Old English cheese spread**
1½ **teaspoons mayonnaise**
½ **teaspoon garlic salt**
½ **teaspoon salt**
1 **7-ounce can crabmeat**
6 **English muffins**

Mix butter, cheese, mayonnaise, garlic salt, salt, and crab together in bowl, combining thoroughly. Cut muffins into small circles using cookie cutter or jigger glass. (Other shapes can be used for variety.) Spread mixture on muffin cutouts. Place under broiler until bubbling.

This recipe can be prepared in advance and kept in the freezer.

Makes about 3 dozen hors d'oeuvres.

SHRIMP MOUSSE

Representative **Patricia Schroeder**—*Colorado*

> 2 envelopes unflavored gelatin
> ½ cup cold water
> 1 10½-ounce can tomato soup (do not dilute)
> 1 medium-sized onion, chopped (about ¾ cup)
> 10 ounces frozen cooked shrimp
> 1 cup mayonnaise
> 2 3-ounce packages cream cheese, softened
> ½ teaspoon salt
>   Dash lemon juice
>   Dash Tabasco sauce
> ¾ cup finely chopped celery
> ½ cup chopped green pepper
> **To serve:**
>   **Assorted crackers**

Soften gelatin in water; set aside. Bring soup to boil. Add softened gelatin, stirring until dissolved. Cool slightly. Place onion, shrimp, mayonnaise, cream cheese, salt, lemon juice and Tabasco in a blender. Blend until smooth. Stir in soup, celery and green pepper. Pour into mold. Refrigerate until set (preferably overnight). Serve with crackers.

Makes 1½ quarts.

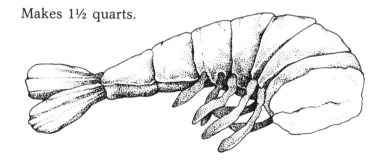

OYSTERS À LA OLIVIER

Representative **Lindy Boggs**—*Louisiana*

    1 tablespoon chopped green onions
    ½ teaspoon minced fresh garlic
    1 8-ounce can mushrooms, drained and chopped
    2 dozen large oysters, shucked
    Flour
 1½ sticks butter, divided
    ½ teaspoon salt
    ½ teaspoon black pepper
    1 wineglass dry sherry (about ⅔ cup)
    1 tablespoon Worcestershire sauce
To serve:
    6 slices buttered toast
    2 tablespoons chopped fresh parsley

Stir together green onions, garlic and mushrooms; set aside. Dry the oysters and powder with flour. In heavy frying pan heat ½ stick butter until bubbly. Quickly brown oysters in butter just until edges curl. Remove from heat.

In another pan, place chopped green onions, garlic, mushrooms and 1 stick butter. Sauté onions lightly. Add salt, pepper, sherry and Worcestershire sauce. Stir until blended. Place oysters on buttered toast, pour sauce over oysters and garnish with chopped parsley.

Makes 4 servings.

AVOCADO AND SHRIMP IN BUTTER SAUCE

Representative **Robert L. Livingston**—*Louisiana*

Good as first course or luncheon salad.

¾ **pound large fresh shrimp**
2 **cups water**
½ **cup dry white wine**
2 **teaspoons white wine vinegar**
1 **medium-sized green onion, cut into 1-inch pieces**
1 **small garlic clove, halved**
½ **cup butter (1 stick)***
To serve:
1 **ripe avocado, at room temperature**
1 **thinly sliced green onion for garnish**

Peel and devein shrimp, but leave tail end part of shell on. In 2-quart saucepan over high heat, heat water to boiling. Add shrimp and let water return to a boil. Lower heat and cook shrimp 2 to 3 minutes, until they are tender and pink; do not overcook. Drain and keep warm.

In same saucepan, combine white wine, wine vinegar, green onion and garlic. Heat mixture to boiling for about 5 minutes or until liquid is reduced to about 2 tablespoons. Discard green onion and garlic. Over medium heat, add butter, 2 tablespoons at a time, beating constantly until butter has melted and mixture has thickened. Keep butter sauce warm.

Peel avocado and cut into 12 wedges. Spoon some butter sauce on small warmed plates. Arrange avocado wedges and a few shrimp. Garnish with green onion. Serve immediately.

*Note: Do not use margarine because sauce will not thicken.

Chapter 2

Salads

MARINATED VEGETABLE SALAD

Representative **Ike Skelton**—*Missouri*

Marinade

- ½ cup apple cider vinegar
- ¼ cup granulated sugar
- 1 cup vegetable or olive oil
- 2 cloves garlic, pressed with garlic press (or mashed)
- ½ cup wine vinegar
- 1 teaspoon dry mustard
- 2 teaspoons salt
- 1 tablespoon dried oregano leaves, crushed
- 1 teaspoon black pepper
- 1 8-ounce bottle Italian dressing

Vegetables

- 2 green peppers, thinly sliced
- 1 cucumber, thinly sliced
- 1 head cauliflower, broken into florets
- 1 bunch broccoli, broken into florets
- 6 carrots, thinly sliced
- 1 pound fresh mushrooms, sliced
- 5 stalks celery, sliced
- 1 bunch green onions, sliced
- 1 dozen cherry tomatoes, halved

Bring vinegar to boil. Add sugar and oil; stir until sugar dissolves. Let mixture cool. Add all remaining marinade ingredients.

Place all prepared vegetables in large noncorrosive bowl or wide-mouthed jar. Pour marinade over vegetables. Cover with plastic wrap. Refrigerate for 24 hours. Stir or turn mixture at least 3 to 4 times during 24-hour period. To serve, drain vegetables and place in clear glass bowl.

Makes 20 servings.

OVERNIGHT
LAYERED GREEN SALAD

Senator **Slade Gorton**—*Washington*

1 medium-sized head iceberg lettuce
1 8-ounce can water chestnuts, drained
½ red or green pepper, seeded
2 stalks celery
1 bunch green onions
1 10-ounce package frozen peas,
  slightly thawed and separated
2 cups mayonnaise
2 teaspoons sugar
½ cup grated Parmesan cheese
1 teaspoon salt
¼ teaspoon garlic powder
¾ pound crisp-fried bacon, crumbled
3 hard-cooked eggs, sliced
2 tomatoes, cut into wedges

If food processor is available, use slicing disc to prepare lettuce, water chestnuts, peppers and celery. Cut up onions with sharp knife. (If food processor is unavailable, shred lettuce and dice water chestnuts, peppers and celery by hand.)

In glass bowl, layer lettuce, water chestnuts, peppers, celery, onions and frozen peas. Mix together mayonnaise, sugar, cheese, salt and garlic powder. Pour over top of layered ingredients. Refrigerate, covered, overnight or longer. Sprinkle top with crumbled bacon and decorate with hard-boiled egg slices and tomato wedges. Serve with tongs or spoon and fork to dig deeply. Will keep several days.

Makes 8 to 10 generous servings.

TOSSED SALAD

Representative **James A. Traficant, Jr.**—*Ohio*

Dressing
> 1 teaspoon dried oregano leaves
> 1 teaspoon black pepper
> 1 teaspoon salt
> 1 tablespoon parsley flakes
> Juice of 1 lemon
> Juice of 1 garlic clove
> Vegetable or olive oil to taste
> Wine vinegar to taste

Salad
> 1 head lettuce (or endive), shredded
> 1 small cucumber, peeled and sliced
> 4 to 6 radishes, halved
> 4 to 6 fresh mushrooms, sliced
> 3 scallions (green part only), minced
> 1 large tomato, sliced
> 1 hard-boiled egg, sliced, for garnish
> ¼ cup blue cheese chunks for garnish

To prepare dressing, combine all ingredients except oil and vinegar in large cruet or jar. Add about ⅔ cup oil and ⅓ to ½ cup vinegar, or to taste. Shake until well blended.

To prepare salad, combine lettuce, cucumber, radishes, mushrooms, scallions, and tomato in large bowl. Add dressing and toss. Garnish with sliced egg and blue cheese.

FRANK AND NANCY'S CAESAR SALAD

Representative **Frank Horton**—*New York*

This is a recipe that Congressman Horton started over 15 years ago. From time to time both he and Mrs. Horton work on improving its taste.

1 clove garlic
2 anchovies
Juice of ½ medium-sized lemon
1 egg
½ cup olive oil
1 tablespoon apple cider vinegar
2 tablespoons wine vinegar
⅛ teaspoon dry mustard
½ teaspoon salt
⅛ teaspoon freshly ground black pepper
⅓ cup grated Parmesan cheese
2 large heads romaine lettuce, torn into pieces and patted dry
1 cup croutons

In small wooden bowl mash garlic, then mash anchovies. Add lemon juice. Warm egg in hot water, separate and add egg yolk to bowl. (Reserve white for another use or discard.) Blend well until mixture is thick and creamy. Slowly add olive oil and beat with spoon until well blended. Add cider vinegar, wine vinegar, mustard, salt, pepper and Parmesan cheese. Blend well.

Arrange dry, crisp romaine in bowl. Add dressing and toss salad just before serving. Add croutons and serve immediately.

Makes 6 servings.

GREEK SALAD

Representative **Michael Bilirakis**—*Florida*

This is a traditional Greek salad that our family and friends have enjoyed for many years.

Dressing
- ½ **cup olive oil**
- ½ **cup wine vinegar**
- 1 **teaspoon salt**
- ¼ **teaspoon black pepper**
- ½ **teaspoon granulated sugar**
- 1 **clove garlic, crushed**
- 1 **teaspoon dried oregano leaves**

Salad
- 1 **small head lettuce**
- 1 **medium-sized tomato, sliced**
- 1 **medium-sized cucumber, sliced**
- 3 **green onions, chopped**
- 1 **small green pepper, cut into strips**
- **Greek black olives**
- **Greek hot salad peppers (from a jar)**
- **Feta cheese, cut into cubes or crumbled**
- **Anchovy fillets (optional), chopped**

Combine all dressing ingredients in jar or cruet. Shake until thoroughly blended. Prepare well in advance and keep refrigerated until ready to use. Makes 1 cup. Shake well before using.

To prepare salad, break lettuce in small pieces. Place in salad bowl with tomato, cucumber, onion and green pepper. Top with black olives, hot green salad peppers, feta cheese, and anchovy fillets if desired. Pour dressing over salad and serve.

Makes 4 servings.

ORIENTAL CABBAGE SALAD

Representative **Sid Morrison**—*Washington*

I wish that I could share some intriguing story about creating this delicious concoction. In fact, it came out of a clear, blue sky on invisible waves of energy. The Gabby Gourmet was on the local radio station as I drove through the majestic Cascade mountains in my district. The recipe sounded good, primarily because I had skipped breakfast that morning. Upon request, the recipe appeared, and my wife and I decided it was delicious, easy to make, and highly nutritious.

2 **packages Top Ramen noodles (chicken flavor), crumbled**
3 to 4 **tablespoons vegetable oil for cooking**
2 **chicken breasts, cooked, boned, skinned and cubed**
½ **medium-sized head cabbage, shredded**
4 **green onions, chopped**
¼ **cup toasted slivered almonds**
2 **tablespoons toasted sesame seeds**
¾ **cup vegetable oil**
3 **tablespoons rice wine vinegar**
2 **tablespoons granulated sugar**
1 **package Top Ramen seasoning mix**
¼ **teaspoon Worcestershire sauce**
Salt to taste
Fresh ground black pepper to taste

In a large fry pan or skillet, sauté noodles in oil. Drain them on paper toweling. In large salad bowl, combine chicken, noodles, cabbage, onions, almonds and sesame seeds. Toss well to blend. In a blender container, combine all remaining ingredients; blend well. Pour mixture over salad ingredients at least 30 minutes before serving. Toss well before serving. Serve over lettuce cups on large plates as an entrée.

Makes 4 servings.

CHINESE SHREDDED CHICKEN SALAD

Representative **Daniel A. Mica**—*Florida*

A luncheon favorite.

4 ounces rice sticks*
  Vegetable oil for cooking
1 large whole chicken, cooked
3 stalks celery, shredded
3 scallions, shredded
1 large head lettuce, shredded
  Sesame seeds for garnish

Dressing

2 tablespoons granulated sugar
¼ cup vegetable oil
1 teaspoon Accent
3 tablespoons wine vinegar
1 teaspoon salt
¼ teaspoon black pepper

Fry rice sticks in oil heated to 425 degrees. Sticks should swell rapidly and become puffy. Do not overcook; they should not brown. These may be prepared ahead and stored in a plastic bag. Shred chicken meat into fine pieces. Combine celery, scallions, and lettuce with chicken.

Combine all dressing ingredients; mix well. Toss salad with dressing; add desired amount of rice sticks. Garnish with toasted sesame seeds.

*Note: Rice sticks are available at Chinese groceries or international food stores.

Makes 6 to 8 servings.

SENATOR JOHNSTON'S FAVORITE CHICKEN SALAD

Senator **J. Bennett Johnston**—*Louisiana*

3 whole chicken breasts (6 halves)
1 1-pound 4-ounce can pineapple chunks, drained (save juice)
1½ cups coarsely chopped celery (not diced, chunkier)
1 cup cashews or walnuts
3 red Delicious apples (unpeeled), chopped in chunks and dipped in pineapple juice to prevent discoloration
Kraft lemon mayonnaise, or use plain mayo mixed with juice of lemons (to taste)

Cook chicken by baking in covered Dutch oven with about 1¼ cups water in preheated 350-degree oven for 45 to 60 minutes. Cool and cut chicken meat into chunks.

Mix all ingredients except mayonnaise in large bowl. Just before serving, toss with mayonnaise. Especially good served with croissants and melon.

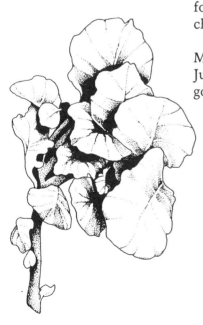

CHICKEN-PASTA SALAD

Representative **Andy Ireland**—*Florida*

Salad
- 8 ounces pasta twists
- Olive oil or vegetable oil
- 2 skinless chicken breasts (whole), poached and cut into strips
- 1 bunch scallions
- 8 ounces fresh snow peas, blanched (or 1 box frozen peas)
- 1 can sliced water chestnuts, drained
- ½ cup sesame seeds, toasted

Dressing
- ½ cup vegetable oil
- ½ cup olive oil
- ½ teaspoon ground ginger
- 2 tablespoons soy sauce
- 3 tablespoons lemon juice
- 1 egg yolk
- 4 tablespoons vermouth
- 2 tablespoons prepared mustard
- 2 tablespoons granulated sugar
- Dash hot pepper sauce (Tabasco)
- ½ cup vegetable oil
- ½ cup olive oil

Cook pasta al dente. Drain well. Combine pasta with a little oil. Cool pasta. Combine pasta and other salad ingredients. Mix all dressing ingredients together except oils. Gradually beat vegetable and olive oil into mixture. Toss dressing and salad until well blended.

Makes 6 servings.

ZITI SALAD

Representative **James A. Traficant, Jr.**—*Ohio*

    1 **pound ziti (or macaroni), cooked and
      cooled**
3 to 4 **large tomatoes (cut in small chunks)**
    1 **can pitted black olives, drained and
      halved**
    2 **medium-sized cucumbers, peeled and
      cut into chunks**
    1 **8-ounce bottle Italian dressing (any
      brand)**
    ½ **2¾-ounce jar Salad Supreme
      (McCormick's)**

Combine all ingredients. Toss well and refrigerate
several hours. Toss again before serving.

SOUTH DAKOTA TACO SALAD

Representative **Tom Daschle**—*South Dakota*

This is a hearty, slightly spicy salad that is a warm-weather favorite.

1 **pound ground beef**
1 **package taco seasoning**
2 **15- to 16-ounce cans red kidney beans, drained**
1 **8-ounce package shredded Cheddar cheese**
1 **head lettuce, cut up**
3 **tomatoes, cut into chunks**
   Approximately 1½ 8-ounce bottles Russian dressing
1 **8-ounce bag taco chips, broken into quarter-size pieces**

Brown ground beef and add taco seasoning following package instructions. Cool overnight or for at least 2 to 3 hours in refrigerator. To cooled ground beef add beans, cheese, lettuce, tomatoes, and enough Russian dressing to make mixture moist (approximately 1½ bottles). Just before serving, add taco chips and mix well. Ground beef can be kept in freezer for a spur of the moment treat.

Makes 12 servings.

PEACH SALAD

Representative **Chalmers Wylie**—*Ohio*

> 1 3-ounce package peach gelatin
> 1½ cups hot water
> 1 8-ounce package cream cheese, softened
> 1 16-ounce can sliced cling peaches, well drained
> 1 10-ounce package frozen raspberries, thawed and drained
> 4 to 5 bananas, cubed

Dissolve gelatin in hot water. Gradually blend into cream cheese until well mixed. Chill until mixture begins to thicken. Then fold in peach slices. Add drained raspberries. Add banana cubes. Chill until set. Serve as salad or dessert with dab of whipped cream.

PORTUGUESE SALAD

Senator **H. J. Heinz, III**—*Pennsylvania*

> 1 **pound salt cod**
> 3 **medium-sized Idaho baking potatoes,**
>   **boiled without peeling and still**
>   **warm**
> 3 **hard-boiled eggs, sliced**
> 1 **bunch green onions, sliced thin, or**
>   1 **small red onion, sliced thin**
>   **Salt to taste**
>   **Fresh black pepper to taste**
> 4 **tablespoons good wine vinegar**
> 1 **cup fruity olive oil (can be vegetable**
>   **oil, if desired)**
>   **Garlic cloves, chopped (optional)**
>   **Tomatoes, cut into wedges and at**
>   **room temperature**
>   **Black and green olives**
>   **Chopped fresh parsley leaves**

To prepare cod for cooking, soak it in water to cover at room temperature for 24 hours, changing water 3 or 4 times. Bring fish slowly to boil in fresh water; drain immediately and pat dry on paper towels. There should be no trace of salt left and texture should be similar to fresh fish except for a slight tendency to shred.

Put prepared salt cod in fresh water, bring to a simmer, and cook very slowly for about 10 minutes. Drain and flake fish. Peel warm potatoes, and slice about ¼-inch thick into a bowl. Add flaked salt cod, hard-boiled eggs, onions, pinch of salt and plenty of fresh ground pepper. Toss with vinaigrette, made from mixing together vinegar and olive oil; do not add all vinaigrette at once as it may be too much. See how much is absorbed by potatoes before adding more. Taste and add more salt if needed. Add some finely chopped garlic, if desired.

Heap salad on a pretty plate. Surround with tomato wedges and olives and sprinkle with a little parsley. Do not refrigerate before serving.

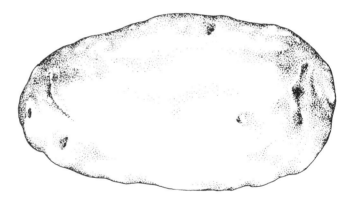

MANDARIN SALAD WITH SWEET AND SOUR DRESSING

Representative **Chalmers Wylie**—*Ohio*

Dressing
- ¼ cup vegetable oil
- 2 tablespoons granulated sugar
- 2 tablespoons apple cider vinegar
- 1 tablespoon snipped fresh parsley leaves
- ½ teaspoon salt
- Dash black pepper
- Dash hot pepper sauce

Salad
- ¼ cup sliced almonds
- 1 tablespoon plus 1 teaspoon granulated sugar
- ¼ head lettuce, torn into bite-sized pieces
- ¼ head romaine lettuce, torn into bite-sized pieces
- 2 medium-sized stalks celery, chopped (about 1 cup)
- 2 green onions with tops, sliced (about 2 tablespoons)
- 1 11½-ounce can mandarin orange segments, drained

To prepare dressing, combine all ingredients in cruet or jar and shake well. Chill until serving time.

Cook almonds and sugar over low heat, stirring constantly until sugar is melted and almonds are coated. Immediately remove pan from heat. Cool and break apart caramelized almonds. Store at room temperature.

Place lettuce and romaine in plastic bag. Add celery and onions. Pour dressing into bag. Add orange segments. Close tightly and shake until well coated. Add almonds and shake; serve immediately.

Makes 4 to 6 servings.

FRESH STRAWBERRY SALAD

Representative **Sam M. Gibbons**—*Florida*
Recipe from: Mrs. Gibbons

2 3-ounce packages strawberry gelatin
2 cups hot water
1½ cups cold water
1 8-ounce package cream cheese
½ cup finely chopped nuts
1 pint fresh strawberries (lightly sugared)

Pour hot water over gelatin and stir well to completely dissolve. Add 1½ cups cold water. Shape cream cheese into balls (using 1 teaspoon for each). Roll in chopped nuts. Place cheese balls evenly spaced in 9-inch ring mold. Cover with lightly sugared strawberries. Pour cooled strawberry gelatin over cheese balls and berries. Chill several hours until gelatin is set. Unmold on large serving plate.

Makes 8 servings.

Chapter 3

Soups and Stews

Soups

Chowders

Chilies

Stews

HOUSE OF REPRESENTATIVES BEAN SOUP

Representative
Thomas P. (Tip) O'Neill, Jr.—*Massachusetts*

Bean Soup has been a featured item on the menu of the House of Representatives Restaurant since long before that day in 1904 when the then Speaker of the House, Joseph G. Cannon, of Illinois, came into the House Restaurant and ordered Bean Soup.

It was typically hot and humid in Washington that day, and, therefore, Bean Soup had been omitted from the menu. "Thunderation," roared Speaker Cannon, "I had my mouth set for Bean Soup. From now on, hot or cold, rain, snow, or shine, I want it on the menu every day."

It has been on the menu every single day since.

We print it herewith, just as it has always been made (adapted to family-size quantity) in the House Restaurant kitchen in the Capitol.

2 **pounds white Michigan beans, washed and sorted**
1 **large ham hock**
  Salt to taste
  Black pepper to taste

Cover beans with cold water and soak overnight. Drain and re-cover with water. Add smoked ham hock and simmer slowly for about 4 hours until beans are tender. Then add salt and pepper. Just before serving, bruise beans with large spoon or ladle, enough to cloud.

Makes 6 servings.

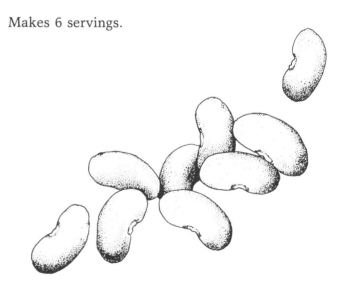

SENATE BEAN SOUP

Representative **Bob Traxler**—*Michigan*
Recipe from: *The Michigan Bean Cookbook*

  1 **pound dry navy beans**
  1 **meaty ham bone, or 1½ pounds ham hocks**
  1 **cup chopped onion**
  2 **garlic cloves, minced**
  1 **cup chopped celery**
  ⅔ **cup mashed potato flakes or 1½ cups mashed potatoes**
  ¼ **cup chopped fresh parsley**
1½ **teaspoons salt**
  1 **teaspoon black pepper**
  1 **teaspoon ground nutmeg**
  1 **teaspoon dried oregano leaves**
  1 **teaspoon dried basil leaves**
  1 **bay leaf**

Wash and sort beans. In large kettle, cover beans with 6 to 8 cups hot water. Bring to boil; boil 2 minutes. Remove from heat, cover and let stand 1 hour. Add another 8 cups cold water and ham bone. Bring to boil; simmer 1½ hours. Stir in remaining ingredients. Simmer 20 to 30 minutes until beans are tender. Remove ham bone, trim off meat, return to soup. Serve hot. Freeze any leftovers, if desired.

Makes about 3 quarts.

SPLIT PEA SOUP

Senator **Alan Cranston**—*California*

> 1 pound dry green split peas
> 1 or 2 ham hocks (or seasoning of your choice)
> 8 cups (2 quarts) water
> 1 medium-sized onion, chopped
> 2 (or more) carrots, peeled and coarsely chopped
> 2 whole garlic cloves
> 2 bay leaves
> 1 teaspoon dried thyme leaves
> Black pepper to taste

Wash peas and ham hocks. Combine with remaining ingredients in a large pot. Bring to a boil. Cover pot, reduce heat and cook for 2 hours. Stir occasionally to prevent peas from sticking to bottom of pot.

Remove ham hocks, garlic and bay leaves. Puree soup using a sieve, food mill or food processor. Return soup to pot, and if necessary, dilute with broth or water.

HEARTY BEEF SOUP

Representative **Rod Chandler**—*Washington*
Recipe from: Mrs. Chandler

Legend has it that Senator Zachariah Chandler enjoyed a similar tasty dish in Michigan. Pioneers of the Chandler family carried it with them to the west where generations of the family have enjoyed it.

1 **pound chopped beef**
1 **cup chopped onion**
3 **cups water**
1 **28-ounce can tomatoes**
1 **cup diced carrots**
1 **cup diced celery**
1 **cup cubed potatoes**
2 **teaspoons salt**
1 **tablespoon bottled brown bouquet sauce**
¼ **teaspoon black pepper**
1 **bay leaf**
⅛ **teaspoon dried basil leaves**

In large saucepan, brown beef, stirring. Drain off fat. Add onions and cook, stirring. Stir in remaining ingredients and heat to boiling. Reduce heat, cover and simmer until vegetables are tender.

Makes 6 servings.

CHARLESTON SHE-CRAB SOUP

Senator **Ernest F. Hollings**—*South Carolina*

Charleston, South Carolina, our home town, is a port city and being such, abounds in seafood cookery. This She-Crab Soup is a particular favorite of ours and we hope you enjoy it too.

2 tablespoons butter
2 teaspoons all-purpose white flour
2 cups whole milk
½ cup cream
½ teaspoon ground mace
¼ teaspoon celery salt
1 tablespoon Worcestershire sauce
1 pound lump crabmeat (with roe if possible)
Salt to taste
Black pepper to taste

To serve:

Sherry (warmed and in a pitcher)

Melt butter in top of double boiler and blend in flour until smooth. Add milk, very slowly, stirring. Add cream. To this add mace, celery salt and Worcestershire sauce. Add crabmeat and fold gently. Heat to piping hot. Add salt and pepper. Pass sherry at table; diners can add it to taste.

Makes 4 to 6 servings.

BROCCOLI OR SPINACH SOUP

Representative **Dan Glickman**—*Kansas*

This recipe has been used by my family for years. Feel free to make your own variation as either way I'm sure you'll enjoy this delicious soup.

1 cup milk
1½ cups light cream
2 tablespoons all-purpose white flour
2 tablespoons butter
1 teaspoon salt
¾ cup cooked broccoli or spinach
1 pinch white or black pepper
4 sprigs parsley
1 cup celery leaves
1 thin slice onion

Place all ingredients in a blender in order given. Blend well. Heat in double boiler, stirring occasionally. May be served hot or cold.

Makes 3 cups.

CHILLED OLIVE-ASPARAGUS SOUP

Representative **Chalmers Wylie**—*Ohio*

1 10-ounce package frozen asparagus
   spears
1 cup boiling water
1 cup sliced leeks, well washed and
   drained
2 tablespoons butter or margarine
1 13 ¾-ounce can chicken broth
½ cup stuffed green Spanish olives
   Dash black pepper
1 cup light cream

Cook asparagus in covered saucepan in boiling water until tender. Place asparagus and liquid in electric blender container. Sauté leeks in butter 2 minutes; add to asparagus and blend until pureed. Pour, along with broth, into saucepan.

Blend olives, pepper and cream in blender until smooth. Add to asparagus mixture. Chill overnight (or heat to serving temperature, stirring frequently, if desired.).

Makes about 5 cups.

COLD CARROT SOUP

Representative **Beverly Byron**—*Maryland*

2 1-pound packages carrots
   Water
1 cup chicken stock (or broth)
1 tablespoon curry powder
1 tablespoon chopped fresh oregano (or
   ½ tablespoon dried oregano leaves)
1 tablespoon chopped fresh coriander
   (or ½ tablespoon dried coriander
   leaves)
1 cup light or heavy cream
   Salt to taste

Peel and coarsely slice carrots. Just barely cover with water and cook until tender. Reserve half of cooking water. In blender in batches, blend carrots with reserved cooking water, chicken stock, curry powder, oregano, coriander and cream. Add salt to taste.

Chill thoroughly before serving.

SANTA FE
FIESTA CUCUMBER SOUP

Senator **Pete Domenici**—*New Mexico*

Delicious and fun.
Garnishes for all tastes.

3 medium-sized cucumbers, peeled and chunked
1 clove garlic
3 cups chicken broth (canned, from cubes or homemade)
3 cups commercial sour cream
1 tablespoon white vinegar
2 teaspoons salt
Assorted garnishes
    Chopped parsley
    Fresh tomatoes, chopped
    Bacon bits
    Croutons
    Thinly sliced green onions, including tops
    Chopped green peppers
    Chopped salted cashews or almonds

Combine cucumbers and garlic in blender. Add a little chicken broth. Whirl until smooth. Then blend in remaining broth. Stir in sour cream. Add white vinegar and salt. Cover and chill thoroughly. Serve in small bowls. Pass around garnishes, each in a different bowl or cup; serve as many or as few as you wish.

GAZPACHO

Senator **Howard M. Metzenbaum**—*Ohio*

3 cups tomato juice
1 medium-sized cucumber, peeled and finely chopped
1 medium-sized green pepper, finely diced
1 medium-sized onion, finely diced
1 clove garlic, chopped
2 tablespoons olive oil
1 tablespoon white wine vinegar
¼ teaspoon Tabasco sauce
½ cup ice water

Garnishes

Toasted croutons
Chopped eggs
Assorted diced vegetables (optional)

Blend all ingredients except garnishes in a blender. Cover and refrigerate; tastes better if made a day ahead. Garnish servings with croutons, chopped eggs, etc.

Makes 4 servings.

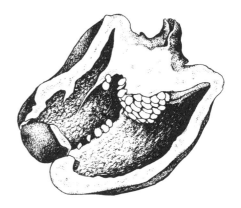

CHINOOK SALMON CHOWDER

Senator **Mark O. Hatfield**—*Oregon*
Recipe from: Antoinette Kuzmanich Hatfield in
More ReMARKable Recipes

    1 **large onion, chopped**
 1½ **cups diced celery**
   ½ **cup (1 stick) butter**
   ½ **cup all-purpose white flour**
    8 **cups (2 quarts) milk**
    8 **7¾-ounce cans Chinook salmon**
    4 **cups cooked potatoes, diced**
    2 **plastic bags frozen mixed vegetables**
    1 **teaspoon dried dillweed**
    1 **tablespoon salt**
To serve:

      Crackers

Sauté onion and celery in butter until onion is tender.
Remove pan from heat and stir in flour until well
blended. Slowly add milk, stirring.

Remove skin and any bones from salmon. Add
salmon along with potatoes, mixed vegetables, dill
and salt. At this point chowder may be frozen.

When ready to serve, cook until vegetables are done.
Serve steaming hot with crackers.

Makes 40 cups.

CAPE COD FISH CHOWDER

Senator **Edward Kennedy**—*Massachusetts*

Even if you have never walked the beach at Cape Cod, the thought conjures up fleets of fishing boats and favorite foods of the Cape. Enjoy this hearty New England favorite!

2 **pounds fresh haddock**
2 **ounces salt pork, diced (or 2**
   tablespoons butter or margarine)
2 **medium-sized onions, sliced**
1 **cup chopped celery**
4 **large potatoes, diced**
1 **bay leaf, crumbled**
1 **quart (4 cups) milk**
2 **tablespoons butter or margarine**
1 **teaspoon salt**
   Freshly ground black pepper to taste

Simmer haddock in 2 cups of water for 15 minutes. Drain off and reserve broth. Remove skin and bones from fish. Sauté diced salt pork in a large pot until crisp. Remove cooked salt pork. Sauté onions in pork fat (or butter) until golden brown. Add fish, celery, potatoes, and bay leaf. Measure reserved fish broth, plus enough boiling water, to make 3 cups liquid. Add to pot and simmer for 30 minutes. Add milk and butter and simmer for an additional 5 minutes or until well heated. Add salt, and pepper to taste.

Makes 8 servings.

NEW ENGLAND CORN CHOWDER

Senator **George J. Mitchell**—*Maine*
Recipe from: Mrs. Mitchell

8 ounces salt pork, diced
2 medium-sized onions, chopped
2 tablespoons all-purpose white flour
4 cups water
6 to 8 medium-sized potatoes, cubed
1 1-pound 1-ounce can cream-style corn
1 12-ounce can evaporated milk
Salt to taste
Black pepper to taste
2 tablespoons butter
Chopped fresh parsley for garnish
Paprika for garnish

In large kettle, cook salt pork until browned and crisp. Remove diced pork and reserve; leave fat in kettle. Add chopped onions and fry in pork fat. Add flour, stirring until blended. Add water and potatoes, making sure water covers potatoes. Bring to a boil. Then simmer, covered, for 15 to 20 minutes, or until potatoes are tender.

Add corn, evaporated milk, salt and pepper to taste, and butter. Heat well but do not boil. Return diced pork to kettle, if you wish, and serve chowder with parsley and paprika.

Makes 2 quarts.

SAVORY SEAFOOD CHOWDER

Representative **Robert Badham**—*California*
Recipe from: Anne Badham

1 6-ounce package frozen king crab (or 7½-ounce can)
1 pound medium-sized peeled shrimp (fresh or frozen)
1 8-ounce can minced clams
4 strips bacon, diced
1 clove garlic, minced
2 cups diced potatoes
1 cup dry white wine
1 teaspoon salt
⅛ teaspoon black pepper
½ teaspoon dried thyme leaves
3 cups milk
1 cup half-and-half
1 16-ounce can creamed corn
½ cup chopped green onions
2 tablespoons minced fresh parsley leaves
Several dashes Tabasco sauce

Drain seafood, reserving liquid. Separate crab. Set aside.

In a large saucepan or kettle, sauté bacon and garlic until bacon is crisp. Add potatoes, reserved liquids from seafoods, wine, salt, pepper, and thyme. Cover and simmer 15 to 20 minutes or until potatoes are tender; stir frequently to prevent potatoes from sticking to bottom of pan. Add crab, shrimp, clams, milk, half-and-half, corn, green onions, parsley, and Tabasco. Heat thoroughly but do not boil.

Makes 6 to 8 servings.

OYSTER STEW
(BACHELOR STYLE)

Representative **Howard Coble**—*North Carolina*

This dish is particularly tasty during the winter months and is particularly easy for us bachelors to prepare.

2 **quarts whole milk**
1 **pint shucked select oysters**
2 **tablespoons butter**
  Salt to taste
  Black pepper to taste

To serve:

  Lots of crackers

Combine all ingredients. Cook over low heat. Heat to simmering, but do not boil. Serve piping hot with crackers.

Note: For a slightly thicker stew, stir 1 or 2 tablespoons all-purpose white flour into a small amount of milk until smooth. Add to pot and heat to piping hot.

JIM WRIGHT'S CHILI

Representative **Jim Wright**—*Texas*

Chili was developed by cowboys as an easily prepared dish that would serve as hearty fare on cattle drives. Some aficionados say that "real" chili should be just chili and meat without any beans; others say that beans give it more substance and make it more interesting. The recipe below is for chili with beans. Chili was made the official State Dish by the Texas Legislature in 1977.

2 **pounds ground beef**
1 **pound bulk pork sausage**
2 **medium-sized onions, chopped**
3 **cloves garlic, chopped**
1 **32-ounce can peeled tomatoes**
2 **15-ounce cans kidney beans**
1 **12-ounce can tomato sauce**
 Chili powder to taste
 Dried oregano leaves to taste
 Cayenne pepper to taste
 Small piece gingerroot, chopped fine
1 **cup tequila**
10 **ground mesquite blossoms**
 Pinch ground sage
 Ground cumin to taste

Brown beef and sausage. Drain off fat from pan. Add all other ingredients. Cook over low flame for 2 to 4 hours.

Makes 6 to 9 servings.

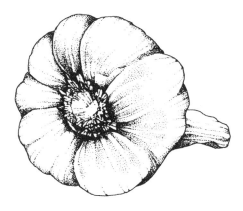

JACK'S HOMEMADE CHILI CON CARNE

Senator **John Danforth**—*Missouri*

3½ pounds top round steak, cut in
   ½-inch cubes
5 tablespoons oil, divided
2 cups coarsely chopped onion
4 cloves garlic, minced
4 tablespoons chili powder
1½ teaspoons dried oregano leaves
1½ teaspoons ground cumin
1 teaspoon crushed dried red pepper
2 cups beef broth
1 1-pound 3-ounce can whole
   tomatoes, including juice
1 6-ounce can tomato paste
1 tablespoon salt
1 teaspoon sugar
3 15-ounce cans kidney or chili beans
1 to 2 tablespoons yellow cornmeal

Pat meat dry with paper towels. Heat 3 tablespoons of oil in a large, heavy pot. When hot, but not smoking, add meat all at once. Sear it until pieces are lightly browned, about 3 to 4 minutes. Use spoon and turn meat constantly. Transfer meat to a bowl. Reduce heat; add remaining 2 tablespoons oil to the pot. Add onion and garlic and sauté until onion is wilted but not browned. Stir in chili powder, oregano, cumin and red pepper; mix well until onions are coated. Add broth, tomatoes, tomato paste, salt and sugar, mixing well. Break up tomatoes with back of spoon. Discard a portion of juice from meat bowl and return meat to pot. Cover and simmer for 1 hour. Uncover and simmer for 40 to 50 minutes. Add beans. Cook briefly, cover and refrigerate overnight.

At serving time, bring chili slowly to a boil and simmer until heated through. Thicken with cornmeal to desired consistency.

AL'S FAVORITE CHILI

Senator **Alan J. Dixon**—*Illinois*

   2 pounds ground chuck
   1 large onion, chopped
   1 large stalk celery, including top, chopped
   ½ medium-sized green pepper, chopped
   2 tomatoes (fresh or canned), chopped
   ½ pound sliced mushrooms
   1 6-ounce can tomato paste
1 to 3 teaspoons chili powder
1 to 2 teaspoons garlic powder
     Salt to taste
     Black pepper to taste
   1 teaspoon granulated sugar or black strap molasses
   1 15-ounce can tomato sauce
   2 scant cups water
   1 teaspoon celery salt
   3 15-ounce cans kidney beans, drained

Brown ground chuck and chopped onion and drain off most fat. Add chopped celery and green pepper. Add remaining ingredients, except kidney beans, and let simmer very gently about 30 minutes. Add kidney beans and simmer gently another 30 minutes.

Makes 8 to 10 servings.

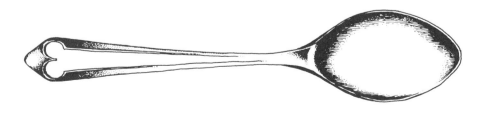

ELECTION DAY CHILI

Representative **Philip Sharp**—*Indiana*

This recipe has become a tradition on election evening in the Sharp family. Since Congressman Sharp's first election to Congress, the chili has been served to family and friends stopping by their home.

   4 **pounds extra-lean ground beef**
   2 **cups finely chopped celery**
   1 **tablespoon onion salt**
   2 **tablespoons salt**
   1 **tablespoon garlic salt**
   1 **tablespoon celery salt**
   4 **medium-sized onions, chopped**
   2 **1-pound 12-ounce cans small red beans (not kidney)**
   4 **1-pound 12-ounce cans tomato sauce**
6 to 8 **tablespoons chili powder (according to taste)**
   2 **46-ounce cans tomato juice**
   4 **tablespoons all-purpose white flour**
   1 **cup cold water**

Brown ground beef in large skillet; drain. Add chopped celery and seasonings. Separately, brown onions until transparent; add to meat mixture. Combine in large cooking container (4-gallon capacity). Perfect container is an electric roaster or 2 large crock pots.

Add red beans, tomato sauce, chili powder and tomato juice, one can at a time. Simmer 3 to 4 hours. About 1 hour before serving time, blend water into flour until smooth. Add mixture gradually to chili. Continue simmering 1 hour longer.

MERAMEC RIVER MUD CHILI

Representative **Robert A. Young**—*Missouri*

In 1947, Irene Slawson took Robert A. Young down along the banks of the Meramec River. He was convinced that this was the woman that he wanted to marry after one taste of Irene's "Meramec River Mud Chili"!

4 **pounds chili meat (chili meat is coarsely ground round steak or well-trimmed beef chuck)**
1 **large onion, chopped**
2 **garlic cloves, minced**
1 **teaspoon ground oregano**
1 **teaspoon cumin seeds**
2 **tablespoons chili powder, or more if desired**
1½ **cups canned whole tomatoes**
2 to 6 **dashes liquid hot pepper sauce**
  Salt to taste
2 **cups hot water**

Place meat, onion, and garlic in large heavy frying pan or Dutch oven. Cook until light-colored. Stir in oregano, cumin seeds, chili powder, tomatoes, hot pepper sauce, salt and hot water. Bring to boil, lower heat and simmer for about 1 hour.

Makes 8 to 10 servings.

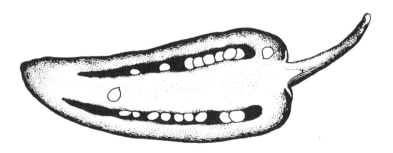

BILL'S MISSOURI CHILI

Representative **Bill Emerson**—*Missouri*

This multiple blue ribbon recipe has been handed down through the Emerson family for many generations.

Vegetable oil
2 pounds ground beef
1 large Bermuda onion, chopped
2 medium-sized green peppers, chopped
Chili powder to taste
Salt to taste
Garlic powder to taste
Black pepper to taste
3 16-ounce cans whole tomatoes
3 16-ounce cans red kidney beans

Cover bottom of cooking pan with oil. Sauté beef, onion and peppers until done. Add seasonings, lower heat, and add tomatoes and beans. Cook for approximately 45 minutes on low heat. Adjust seasonings to taste.

Makes 8 servings.

CHILI CON "CONTE"

Representative **Silvio Conte**—*Massachusetts*

Bacon fat for sautéing
6 onions, chopped
2 pounds ground sirloin
2 3-pound 6-ounce cans red kidney
   beans, drained
1 quart tomatoes, chopped (I prefer my
   home-grown)
4 teaspoons chili powder
Pinch dried thyme leaves
2 teaspoons chopped fresh parsley
3 cloves garlic, chopped
Pinch dried basil leaves
Pinch ground allspice
1 stick butter
2 medium-sized green peppers,
   chopped
1 cup red wine
Small jar chili peppers, chopped
½ can jalapeño peppers, chopped

Sauté onions in bacon fat, or other meat drippings. Brown meat; add beans and remaining ingredients. Simmer gently for a few hours. Refrigerate overnight. When ready to serve, remove all congealed fat, and reheat.

Makes about 4 quarts.

OLD-FASHIONED GEORGIA BRUNSWICK STEW

Representative **Richard Ray**—*Georgia*

1 **fat hen (or 4- to 5-pound roasting chicken)**
1 **medium-sized fresh pork roast (about 4 to 4½ pounds)**
4 **medium-sized Irish potatoes**
2 **cups white peas**
2 **cups green peas, small ones preferred**
2 **cups butter beans (or baby lima beans)**
2 **large chopped onions (Vidalia variety, if available)**
1 **quart tomatoes**
1 **28-ounce bottle ketchup**
4 **tablespoons Worcestershire sauce**
¼ **cup lemon juice**
  Salt to taste
  Black pepper to taste
  Garlic to taste

Cook meat in water to cover until it is falling off bones. Remove bones and skin. Shred meat into small pieces. To the broth, add vegetables, meat and all seasonings. Cook slowly for about 4 to 6 hours, stirring occasionally.

Good served with barbecue.

BRAZOS RIVER STEW

Representative **Tom DeLay**—*Texas*

3 slices bacon
1 pound stew beef cubes
1 16-ounce can tomatoes
2 cups beef broth or bouillon
1 cup water
2 stalks celery, sliced
2 medium-sized onions, chopped
2 garlic cloves, minced
1 ounce (2 tablespoons) Worcestershire
   sauce
1 teaspoon chili powder
1 tablespoon all-purpose white flour
   Salt to taste
   Black pepper to taste
4 medium-sized carrots, coarsely sliced
4 small potatoes, peeled
1 8-ounce can niblets corn

Fry bacon in a Dutch oven or large stew pot. Remove bacon strips and drain on paper towel; leave fat in pot. Add stew meat to pot and sear. Lower heat and add tomatoes, beef broth, water, celery, onion, garlic, Worcestershire sauce and chili powder. Cover and simmer 2 hours.

Remove ¼ cup broth from stew, cool and mix with flour. Add flour mixture to stew. Add salt and pepper as needed. Add carrots and potatoes and cook 30 minutes. Add corn and crumbled bacon strips; cook another 5 minutes. Serve in large bowls.

Makes 5 to 6 servings.

MARYLAND KIDNEY STEW

Senator **Charles McC. Mathias, Jr.**—*Maryland*

This is a favorite Sunday morning breakfast in Maryland.

1 **pair beef kidneys**
¼ **cup (½ stick) butter**
1 **medium-sized onion, chopped**
3 **tablespoons all-purpose white flour**
2 **quarts (8 cups) hot water**
Salt to taste
Black pepper to taste

To serve:

Waffles or hotcakes

Soak kidneys in cold salted water for 1 hour. Remove gristle and cut meat into small pieces.

Place butter in skillet and melt. Add onions and flour. Cook, stirring constantly, until golden brown. Add water and cut-up kidney meat. Simmer from early morning until evening, allowing 2 hours to first come to a boil. (More water may be required if the gravy thickens too much.) On the following morning, again bring to a boil. Season to taste with salt and pepper. Serve over waffles or hotcakes.

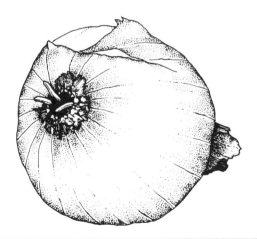

Chapter 4

Side Dishes

Vegetables

Potatoes

Grains

Pasta

Beans

CREAMED ASPARAGUS

Representative **Lee Hamilton**—*Indiana*

> 1 **cup fresh asparagus tips, lightly cooked**
> 3 **hard-cooked eggs, peeled and sliced**
> 1 **cup buttered bread crumbs**
> 1 **cup medium white sauce (use juice from asparagus for half of liquid)**
> ¾ **cup grated Cheddar cheese**

Arrange following in greased baking dish: layer of asparagus, sliced eggs, and buttered crumbs. Add cheese to white sauce. Pour white sauce over top of casserole.

Bake in preheated 350-degree oven until sauce is heated through and crumbs are brown, approximately 20 to 25 minutes.

Makes 4 to 6 servings.

INDIAN-STYLE VEGETABLES

Representative **Barbara B. Kennelly**—*Connecticut*

> 1 medium-sized onion, chopped
> 2 tablespoons vegetable oil
> 2 large potatoes, peeled and cubed
> 2 carrots, peeled and chopped
> 4 medium-sized tomatoes, peeled and quartered
> 1 medium-sized head cauliflower, separated into florets
> 1 medium-sized eggplant, cubed
> ½ teaspoon black pepper
> ¼ teaspoon ground ginger
> 1 teaspoon curry powder
> 1 tablespoon salt
> ½ teaspoon ground cumin
> ⅛ teaspoon ground cayenne pepper
> 1 to 1½ cups water

In a large saucepan or Dutch oven, sauté onion in oil 4 minutes or until soft. Add all remaining ingredients. Bring to boil. Lower heat, cover and simmer 30 minutes or until vegetables are tender.

This recipe can also be prepared ahead, and either refrigerated or frozen in cooking liquid. Before refrigerating, or freezing, allow to cool first. At serving time, simply reheat, drain, and serve hot.

Makes 8 servings.

ITALIAN ZUCCHINI CASSEROLE

Representative **Elwood H. Hillis**—*Indiana*

> 5 **cups thinly sliced unpeeled zucchini**
> ¾ **cup chopped onion**
> ½ **cup butter**
> 2 **eggs**
> 1 **8-ounce package shredded mozzarella cheese**
> ½ **teaspoon salt**
> ½ **teaspoon black pepper**
> ¼ **teaspoon garlic powder**
> ¼ **teaspoon dried basil leaves**
> ¼ **teaspoon dried oregano leaves**
> 1 **8-ounce can Pillsbury crescent rolls**
> 1 **tablespoon Dijon mustard**

Cook zucchini and onion in butter for about 10 minutes in large skillet. Remove from heat. Blend together remaining ingredients, except rolls and mustard. Stir mixture into vegetables.

Separate dough into 8 triangles. Place in ungreased 9- x 13-inch baking pan and press over bottom and up sides. Spread dough with Dijon mustard. Pour vegetable mixture into crust. Bake in preheated 375-degree oven for 20 minutes.

Makes 10 to 12 servings.

SCALLOPED EGGPLANT

Representative **Ralph Regula**—*Ohio*

1 medium-sized eggplant, peeled and
  cubed
  Salt to taste
3 tablespoons grated onion
1 10½-ounce can cream of mushroom
  soup
1 cup grated sharp cheese
¾ cup buttered bread crumbs
  Butter

Peel and cube eggplant. Cook eggplant until just tender in boiling salted water. Drain well.

Place eggplant in baking dish. Sprinkle grated onion over it. Cover with mushroom soup. Top with ½ cup grated cheese. Top with buttered bread crumbs. Dot crumbs with butter. Sprinkle remaining cheese over top. Bake in preheated 350-degree oven for 45 minutes until nicely browned.

Makes 4 servings.

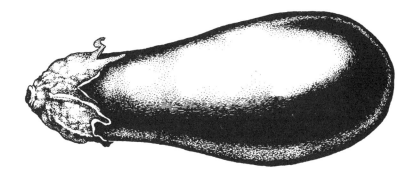

MARINATED GREEN BEANS

Senator **Pete Wilson**—*California*
Recipe from: Mrs. Wilson

> 2 **pounds fresh green beans**
> 3 **tablespoons coarse (kosher-style) salt, divided**
> 2 **teaspoons mustard seeds**
> 2 **teaspoons dillweed**
> 2 **teaspoons crushed small dried hot chili peppers**
> 2 **teaspoons dill seeds**
> 4 **cloves garlic, peeled**
> 2 **cups water**
> 2 **cups white vinegar**
> ⅔ **cup granulated sugar**

Snip ends from beans and wash thoroughly; leave whole or cut in half if long. In a large pan bring 2 quarts of water to boil; add 1 tablespoon salt and beans. Let water return to a boil and cook beans, uncovered, for about 5 minutes or until beans are just tender-crisp. Drain immediately and cool.

Pack beans into 4 1-pint refrigerator containers (or jars). Into each container put ½ teaspoon each mustard seeds, dillweed, chili peppers and dill seeds, and 1 clove garlic.

Combine 2 cups water, vinegar, sugar, and remaining 2 tablespoons salt in a saucepan. Bring to a boil. Pour mixture over beans. Cool, cover, and chill overnight or as long as two weeks.

Note: Instead of beans, you can use about 2 pounds of carrots or cauliflower, or a mixture of these and beans. Peel carrots and cut into thin sticks; separate cauliflower into florets; reduce cooking time to 3 minutes, or until tender.

COPPER CARROT PENNIES

Representative **Tim Penny**—*Minnesota*

>   2 1-pound bags carrots, peeled and
>   sliced
>   1 medium-sized green pepper, sliced in
>   rings or diced
>   1 medium-sized onion, sliced in rings
>   or diced

Marinade

>   1 10½-ounce can tomato soup
>   1 cup granulated sugar
>   ¾ cup apple cider vinegar
>   ½ cup vegetable oil
>   1 teaspoon dry mustard
>   1 teaspoon Worcestershire sauce
>   Salt to taste
>   Black pepper to taste

Boil carrots in salted water until just tender. Drain
and cool. In bowl, alternate layers of carrots, peppers
and onions. Combine marinade ingredients in jar and
shake to blend. Pour over vegetables. Cover and
refrigerate. Better if allowed to marinate overnight.

MARGARET CHILES' FRIED CORN

Senator **Lawton Chiles**—*Florida*

This is Senator Chiles' favorite recipe.

> 6 **strips bacon**
> 10 **fresh ears corn, shucked**
> 3 **tablespoons butter**
> **Milk as needed**
> **Salt to taste**
> **Black pepper to taste**

Fry bacon, set aside. Leave fat from bacon in skillet.

Prepare corn as follows: Hold ear perpendicular to cutting board. With sharp knife, slice downward, cutting off tip ends of kernels—then scrape milk out of remaining kernels.

Heat bacon fat in skillet. Add scraped corn and kernel tips. Fry lightly for about 3 minutes, stirring constantly. Add enough milk to make creamed corn consistency. Add 3 tablespoons butter. Cook another 5 minutes. Add salt and pepper to taste. Pour in serving dish and sprinkle crushed bacon bits over all.

Makes 6 servings.

FRIED OKRA

Representative **Bill Lehman**—*Florida*

One of my favorite recipes!

6 strips bacon, diced
1 pound fresh okra, tops removed
2 medium-sized fresh tomatoes
1 large onion, diced

Cook bacon in large skillet until almost done. Add okra, tomatoes and onions to skillet. Sauté until okra is tender, stirring frequently; break up okra with a spoon while cooking.

Makes 4 to 6 servings.

SQUASH SOUFFLÉ

Senator **Warren Rudman**—*New Hampshire*

1 **cup all-purpose white flour**
½ **cup granulated sugar**
2 **12-ounce packages frozen winter squash, thawed**
6 **eggs**
2 **cups milk**
Salt to taste
Ground nutmeg to taste
½ **stick butter, melted**

Combine flour and sugar and stir until well blended. Stir mixture into squash. Whisk eggs into squash mixture, one at a time; whisk very well otherwise eggs will not be even throughout. Stir in all remaining ingredients. Put in greased 1-quart soufflé or baking dish. Bake 65 to 70 minutes in preheated 350-degree oven. Soufflé holds very well.

Makes 4 to 6 servings.

Side Dishes

MARY'S SWEET POTATOES WITH CARAMEL SAUCE

Senator **Jim Sasser**—*Tennessee*

4 cups cooked, peeled, and mashed
    sweet potatoes
¾ cup brown sugar, packed
1 teaspoon vanilla extract
½ cup cream (or half and half)
1 cup pecans, chopped
Sauce
1 cup butter
1 cup granulated sugar
½ cup cream
    Pinch salt
1 teaspoon vanilla extract

After mashing potatoes, add brown sugar, vanilla and
½ cup cream. Put in greased casserole. Make a
"well" in center and sprinkle top with pecans. Bake
in preheated 350-degree oven until hot.

Meanwhile, prepare sauce: Melt butter and
granulated sugar together in iron skillet until golden.
Slowly pour in ½ cup cream and cook about 2
minutes; be careful of splattering. Add salt and
vanilla. Just before serving pour sauce over sweet
potatoes, filling up well.

Makes 6 servings.

SWEET POTATOES IN ORANGE CUPS

Representative **Richard Ray**—*Georgia*

2 **pounds cooked, mashed sweet potatoes**
1 **stick butter, melted**
3 **eggs, slightly beaten**
¾ **cup granulated sugar**
1 **cup brown sugar, packed**
1 **teaspoon ground cinnamon**
1 **teaspoon ground nutmeg**
1 **teaspoon vanilla extract**
6 **medium-sized oranges, halved, pulp removed and juice reserved**
1 **cup orange juice (reserved from oranges)**
12 **marshmallows**

Combine mashed potatoes with butter and eggs. Beat with electric mixer (to give a creamy texture). Add remaining ingredients, except orange shells and marshmallows. Fill orange shells with mixture and place in a 12-cup muffin tin.

Bake in preheated 400-degree oven for about 30 minutes. Top each cup with marshmallow and brown lightly. Serve hot.

Makes 12 servings.

BOURBON
SWEET POTATOES

Representative **Robert H. Michel**—*Illinois*

> 4 **pounds sweet potatoes, boiled until tender, peeled and mashed**
> 1 **stick butter**
> ½ **cup bourbon**
> ⅓ **cup orange juice**
> ¼ **cup brown sugar, packed**
> 1 **teaspoon salt**
> ½ **teaspoon apple pie spice (cinnamon and nutmeg combined)**
> ⅓ **cup chopped pecans**

Combine sweet potatoes with all remaining ingredients, except pecans, beating. Place in casserole. Ring casserole top with pecans. Bake in preheated 350-degree oven for 45 minutes or until done.

Makes 12 or more servings.

CORN PUDDING CASSEROLE

Representative **Harold L. Volkmer**—*Missouri*

Corn Pudding Casserole has been a long-time favorite in my family.

½ cup chopped onion
¼ cup chopped green pepper
1 stick margarine
1 16-ounce can cream-style corn
1 16-ounce can whole kernel corn, including juice
3 eggs, beaten
Salt to taste
Black pepper to taste
1 package Jiffy corn muffin mix

Sauté onion and green pepper in margarine for 5 minutes. Stir all ingredients into muffin mix; beat until smooth. Bake in casserole in preheated 350-degree oven for 30 to 40 minutes. (Longer baking makes pudding firmer.)

Makes 6 servings.

KUGELIS
(POTATO CASSEROLE)

Representative **Richard J. Durbin**—*Illinois*

Kugelis is an authentic Lithuanian potato side dish. My mother, Ann Durbin, came to this country from Lithuania as a child. Her mother, who was the family's sole support, had to be very frugal with family finances.

My mother feasted on this delicious, yet inexpensive, dish many times while she was growing up in East St. Louis. (East St. Louis is a town in Illinois.) Although this recipe is not her mother's, she tested many kugelis recipes before finding the best one in a very old Lithuanian cookbook.

Anyone who tries this recipe will not be disappointed . . . or hungry!

10 **large red potatoes**
1 **large onion**
5 **strips bacon, diced**
½ **cup hot milk or evaporated milk**
3 **eggs**
2 **teaspoons salt**
¼ **teaspoon black pepper**

Peel and grate potatoes. (A food processor makes this job easy.) Grate onion. Fry diced bacon until crisp; pour bacon fat and bacon over potatoes. Add hot milk. Add eggs one at a time, beating. Add salt and pepper and mix well. Pour into greased 9- x 13-inch baking pan. Bake in preheated 400-degree oven for 15 minutes. Reduce heat to 375 and bake for 45 minutes or until firm when tested by inserting a knife in center.

COMPANY POTATO CASSEROLE

Senator **Steven D. Symms**—*Idaho*
Recipe from: Fran Symms

> 2 **pounds frozen hash brown potatoes**
> ½ **stick butter or margarine, melted**
> 1 **10½-ounce can cream of mushroom soup**
> 1 **cup commercial sour cream**
> 2 **tablespoons minced green onions**
> 1½ **cups grated Cheddar cheese**
> **Salt to taste**
> **Black pepper to taste**
> ½ to 1 **cup crushed cornflakes**

Mix all ingredients except cornflakes together and put in large greased casserole. Sprinkle corn flakes over top. Bake 1 hour in preheated 350-degree oven.

Makes 8 servings.

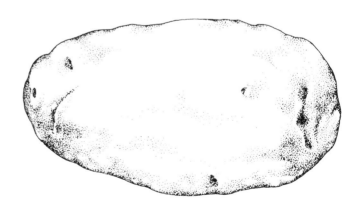

QUICK AND EASY SCALLOPED POTATOES

Representative **Richard Stallings**—*Idaho*

1 **8-ounce package cream cheese**
1 **10½-ounce can cream of chicken or cream of mushroom soup**
¼ **cup finely chopped onion**
¾ **package frozen (Idaho) hash brown potatoes**
1 **cup grated Cheddar cheese**

Mix and heat together cream cheese and soup in large saucepan. Add onion and mix well. Add frozen potatoes, which have been broken up with a spoon. Mix well. Place in a 1½-quart casserole and top with grated cheese. Bake in preheated 350-degree oven for 45 minutes.

SOUPER EASY, BEEFY RICE CASSEROLE

Representative **Connie Mack**—*Florida*
Recipe from: Priscilla Mack

This recipe has been handed down in our family for years. A dear friend in Ft. Myers, Florida, first served this dish to my family.

1 10½-ounce can Campbell's onion soup
1 10½-ounce can Campbell's beef broth
1 stick butter or margarine, softened
1 4-ounce can mushrooms (stems and pieces), drained
1 cup uncooked white rice

Stir together all ingredients in a casserole dish. Cover and bake in preheated 375-degree oven for 1 hour.

Makes 4 servings.

FETTUCCINE TOSS-UP

Representative **Dante B. Fascell**—*Florida*

This is one of our family favorites. Buon appetito!

1 pint fresh mushrooms, thinly sliced (1½ to 2 cups sliced)
2 cloves garlic, peeled
1 stick butter, melted
¾ to 1 pound zucchini, cut julienne style (into matchstick strips)
1 cup heavy cream
1 pound cooked fettuccine, well drained and still hot
½ cup chopped fresh parsley leaves
1 cup grated romano cheese
  Salt to taste
  Black pepper to taste
¾ cup diced cooked chicken or ham, or 4 strips crisp crumbled bacon (optional)

Sauté mushrooms and garlic in melted butter for 2 to 3 minutes. Remove garlic and discard. Add zucchini and cream and simmer for 5 minutes.

Combine hot fettuccine, parsley, cheese, salt and pepper in a serving bowl. Toss well. Add the mushroom-zucchini-cream mixture. Toss again. If desired, chicken, ham or bacon may also be included. Add to mushrooms along with zucchini and cream.

PASTA ALLA CHECCA (COLD PASTA WITH TOMATO SAUCE)

Representative **Ed Zschau**—*California*

2 pounds ripe Italian plum tomatoes (if substituting other tomatoes, use 6 medium-sized, firm but very ripe ones)

¼ cup salt-packed capers, rinsed and patted dry

1 cup pitted black olives (Gaeta, if possible), halved

40 fresh basil leaves, patted dry and torn into pieces

½ cup extra-virgin olive oil, divided
Coarse salt to taste
Freshly ground black pepper to taste

1 clove garlic, crushed or chopped

1 pound ribbed rigatoni, mezzi ditali, conchiglie, or similar pasta
About 1 cup squid

2 tablespoons lemon juice

Dip tomatoes in boiling water for 1 minute; peel and dice, discarding seeds. Place diced tomatoes in bowl large enough to hold pasta. Add capers, olives, basil leaves, ¼ cup olive oil, salt and pepper. Add garlic. (If crushed, remove before serving.) Place mixture in sun for 2 to 3 hours, if possible. Otherwise, leave at room temperature for 3 or 4 hours.

Bring 4 quarts water and 1½ tablespoons salt to boil in large pasta pot, and cook pasta until very al dente, just barely cooked through. Pour 2 cups cold water into pot to stop cooking process; drain pasta. Add remaining ¼ cup olive oil to pasta; mix well. Add pasta to tomato sauce mixture and toss again.

Clean and wash squid. Acidulate in water with lemon juice. Bring 2 quarts water to boiling. Add squid. Simmer 30 seconds. Remove and cool under cold water. Slice into ½-inch sections. Add to pasta.

Note: If serving cold, let pasta cool at room temperature before adding tomato sauce at last minute. Two teaspoons dried basil leaves may be substituted for fresh basil.

BAKED GRITS
WITH CHEESE

Representative **Lindy Boggs**—*Louisiana*

1½ **cups grits**
6 **cups water**
2½ **teaspoons salt**
1 **stick butter**
½ **teaspoon cayenne pepper**
3 **eggs, beaten**
8 **ounces sharp cheese, grated**
6 **ounces roll garlic cheese, chopped**

Add grits to boiling salted water and cook until done. Add butter, cayenne, beaten eggs, 6 ounces sharp cheese, and 6 ounces garlic cheese, mixing well. Pour into buttered 2½ quart baking dish. Sprinkle top with remaining 2 ounces sharp cheese. Bake 1 hour 15 minutes in preheated 350-degree oven.

Note: This may be prepared ahead. Keep refrigerated and bake before serving.

CORNBREAD STUFFING

Representative **Bill Archer**—*Texas*
Recipe from: Sharon Archer

> 1 cup hot chicken broth (or broth from cooked giblets)
> 8 slices stale bread, broken into pieces (or about 2 cups)
> 1 cup packed crumbled cornbread
> ½ cup chopped celery
> ½ cup chopped onion
> Butter or margarine
> ½ cup chopped fresh parsley
> 2 eggs, beaten
> 1 cup chopped pecans
> ¾ teaspoon salt
> ¼ teaspoon black pepper
> 1 teaspoon poultry seasoning
> 4 hard-boiled eggs, chopped

Pour broth over bread crumbs and cornbread and let stand until softened. Sauté celery and onions in butter until tender. Combine bread mixture with celery, onions, parsley, raw eggs, salt, pepper, chopped pecans and poultry seasoning. Mix well and add cooked eggs.

Bake in preheated 350-degree oven in greased casserole for 30 minutes or stuff into turkey.

Note: Oysters sautéed in butter until just cooked through can also be added to dressing.

Makes 8 to 10 servings.

KIKA'S RIO GRANDE CHILI BEANS

Representative **E. (Kika) de la Garza**—*Texas*

1 **pound dry pinto beans**
1 **pound lean ground beef**
1 **large onion, chopped**
1 **8-ounce can tomato sauce**
1 **16-ounce can stewed tomatoes, chopped**
6 **tablespoons chili powder**
1½ **teaspoons ground cumin**
3 **cloves garlic, chopped**
Salt to taste
Hot chilies or Tabasco sauce to taste

Clean and wash beans. Place in large pot and cover with cold water. Let soak overnight. Next day, heat pot to boiling. Reduce heat and simmer, covered, for 30 minutes.

Brown meat in frying pan and drain. Add remaining ingredients to meat and mix. Then add to beans and cook over low heat until beans are tender, about 1 hour longer.

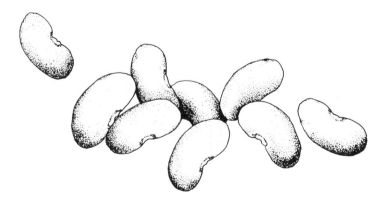

Chapter 5

Main Dish Casseroles Lunch & Supper Entrées

Casseroles

Soufflés

Savory Pies

Sandwiches

PRESIDENT REAGAN'S FAVORITE MACARONI AND CHEESE

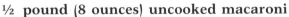

President **Ronald Reagan**

½ **pound (8 ounces) uncooked macaroni**
1 **teaspoon butter**
1 **egg, beaten**
1 **teaspoon dry mustard**
1 **teaspoon salt**
1 **cup milk**
3 **cups grated sharp cheese**

Boil macaroni in water until tender and drain thoroughly. Stir in butter and egg. Mix mustard and salt with 1 tablespoon hot water and add to milk; set aside. Add cheese to macaroni, reserving enough cheese to sprinkle on top. Pour into greased casserole; add milk, sprinkle with reserved cheese.

Bake in preheated 350-degree oven for about 45 minutes or until custard is set and top is crusty.

AUNT EDA'S NEVER FAIL CHEESE SOUFFLÉ

Representative **Don Bonker**—*Washington*

½ cup soft bread crumbs
½ cup evaporated milk
½ cup water
¼ cup butter
½ teaspoon salt
½ teaspoon dry mustard
1 cup grated cheese
3 eggs, separated and beaten

Add crumbs to milk and water and bring to a boil. Add butter, seasonings and cheese; mix well. Add beaten egg yolks and beat over heat. Remove from heat and fold in beaten egg whites. Place in greased dish. Place this dish in larger pan that is filled about ¼ to ⅓ full of warm water.

Bake in preheated 375-degree oven for 30 to 40 minutes.

SUNDAY BRUNCH CASSEROLE

Senator **Jay Rockefeller**—*West Virginia*
Recipe from: Carolanne Griffith, in *MOUNTAIN MEASURES: A Second Serving,* a collection of West Virginia recipes.

> 4 **cups day-old bread, cubed**
> 2 **cups grated Cheddar cheese**
> 10 **eggs, lightly beaten**
> 4 **cups milk**
> 1 **teaspoon dry mustard**
> 1 **teaspoon salt**
> ¼ **teaspoon onion powder**
> **Dash black pepper**
> 8 to 10 **strips cooked bacon, crumbled**
> ½ **cup sliced cooked or canned mushrooms**
> ½ **cup peeled and chopped tomatoes**

Place bread in bottom of a greased 2-quart casserole. Sprinkle with cheese. Beat next 6 ingredients together. Pour over cheese and bread. Sprinkle with bacon, mushrooms and tomatoes. Refrigerate, covered, up to 24 hours. Bake, uncovered, in preheated 325-degree oven 1 hour or until set.

Makes 8 servings.

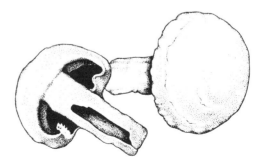

CHILIES AND CHEESE CASSEROLE

Representative **Beverly Byron**—*Maryland*

> 2 **4-ounce cans green chilies, drained and chopped**
> 3 **cups grated Monterey Jack cheese**
> 2 **medium-sized tomatoes, sliced**
> 4 **eggs**
> 1 **cup heavy cream**
> ¾ **cup all-purpose flour**
> 1 **teaspoon salt**
>
> **To serve:**
>
> > **Commercial sour cream**
> > **Diced avocados and chopped onions (or green onions)**

Layer greased casserole with green chilies, then cheese. Top with tomato slices.

Beat together eggs, cream, flour and salt until well mixed. Pour over tomato slices. Bake in preheated 350-degree oven for 1 hour. Serve cut into squares, garnished with sour cream, avocados and chopped onions.

GREEN CHILI ENCHILADAS

Representative **Tom DeLay**—*Texas*

        1 large onion, finely chopped
        1 tablespoon margarine
       12 corn tortillas, cut into quarters
        1 10½-ounce can cream of chicken
          soup
        ½ cup commercial sour cream
        1 4-ounce can green chilies, drained
          and chopped
        2 cups diced, cooked chicken meat
          (from 1 whole chicken)
  2 to 3 cups grated cheese

Lightly sauté onion in margarine; set aside. Cover bottom of 2-quart casserole with tortilla pieces.

Stir together soup with ½ cup water and sour cream. Add green chilies, chicken and sautéed onion. Cover tortilla pieces with some of chicken mixture. Then cover with some of cheese. Repeat layering about 2 or 3 times, ending with cheese. Bake in preheated 350-degree oven for 30 minutes.

Makes 4 servings.

RUDD'S CHILAQUILES

Representative **Eldon Rudd**—*Arizona*

> 12 **corn tortillas**
> 1 **16-ounce can tomatoes**
> 2 to 3 **chilies (green chilies or serranos)**
> ½ **medium-sized onion, chopped**
> 1 **garlic clove, chopped (optional)**
> **Salt to taste**
> **Black pepper to taste**
> 1 **cup grated Cheddar cheese**
> **Commercial sour cream for garnish**

Cut tortillas into bite-sized pieces. Fry and drain them. Place tortilla pieces in shallow casserole. Combine tomatoes, chilies, onion, and seasonings in saucepan. Boil 15 minutes. Pour mixture over tortillas and top with grated cheese. Mixture in casserole should be no more than 1 inch thick. Bake in preheated 350-degree oven, 30 minutes. Garnish with sour cream. May be frozen.

Variation: Browned ground beef or cooked chicken, chopped, may be added before baking. You can substitute 2 7½-ounce cans green chili salsa for tomatoes and chilies.

Makes 4 to 6 servings.

TORTILLA À LA PAISANA

Representative **Martin Frost**—*Texas*
Recipe from: Valerie Frost

2 medium-sized red potatoes
Salt to taste
1 medium-sized onion, finely chopped
Olive oil (Spanish, if possible; Italian is too heavy)
Corn oil
4 or 5 eggs
1 small can small peas, drained (don't use whole can)
1 small jar mushroom pieces, drained
1 small jar pimientoes, drained and chopped

Use potato peeler to peel, then finely slice the potatoes, as if for potato chips. Salt the potatoes. Heat a mixture of half Spanish olive oil and corn oil (about 1½ inch deep) in bottom of pan to almost smoky hot temperature. Pile in potatoes and onion and let cook without stirring for about 7 or 8 minutes. (Potatoes and onions should be covered by oil.) Use slotted spoon to turn up underneath layers and break up potato pieces. Cook about 15 to 20 minutes.

Meanwhile, ready eggs. Beat eggs and add whatever proportion of mushrooms, pimientoes, and peas you want. (Don't use whole can of peas; the tortilla won't hold together very well.) When potatoes are soft and golden and onion is transparent remove pan from heat. Drain off oil. Combine cooked potatoes and onions in bowl with egg mixture and mix by hand until evenly distributed. Put a little oil in pan. When hot, pour mixture in. Use spoon to pull up on sides of mixture while cooking (medium heat) so that more flows to bottom of pan to cook. After about 5 minutes remove from heat, put a plate over pan, and flip tortilla onto plate. Slide upside-down tortilla back into pan (first spoon a bit more oil in pan), with a shuffleboard-type motion. Push on mixture while cooking to get moisture out of middle. Cook for about 5 minutes. Remove by putting a clean plate over pan and flipping. Tortilla will take shape of pan. It should be a golden-brown color. (¡Qué pinta más bonita!)

Serve with lettuce and tomato salad with vinegar/oil dressing and hard rolls. Tortilla should be cut in wedges, and can be eaten cold. It can also be cut into cubes for parties.

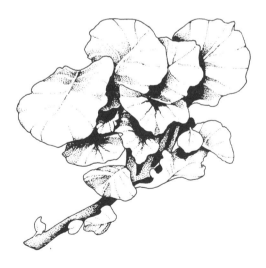

CHICKEN TUJAGUE

Representative **Lindy Boggs**—*Louisiana*

- 10 chicken breast halves, cooked and cut up
- 4 cups diced celery
- 2½ cups mayonnaise
- 1½ cups slivered toasted almonds
- 1½ tablespoons salt
- 2 cans sliced mushrooms, well drained and sautéed
- 2 tablespoons Worcestershire sauce
- ½ pound sharp Cheddar cheese, diced or shredded
- Crumbled potato chips for garnish
- 1 teaspoon paprika

Mix all ingredients except potato chips and paprika together. Sprinkle crumbled potato chips and paprika on top. Bake 20 minutes in preheated 400-degree oven.

Makes 6 to 8 servings.

CHICKEN-BROCCOLI CASSEROLE

Representative **William S. Broomfield**—*Michigan*

4 whole chicken breasts
1 medium-sized onion
1 small stalk celery
1 small carrot
 Salt to taste
 Black pepper to taste
2 9- to 10-ounce packages frozen
  broccoli
1 10½-ounce can cream of chicken
  soup
⅔ cup mayonnaise
⅓ cup evaporated milk
½ cup grated Cheddar cheese
1 teaspoon lemon juice
½ teaspoon curry powder
1 cup bread crumbs

Skin chicken breasts. Poach in water or chicken broth, adding onion, celery, carrot, salt and pepper to liquid. Cook, bone, and cut meat into pieces. Cook broccoli according to package directions.

In greased 9 x 13-inch oven proof flat casserole lay out cooked broccoli. Top with chicken meat. Combine soup with mayonnaise, milk, cheese, lemon juice, and curry powder. Pour mixture over chicken and broccoli. Top with crumbs, cover and bake for 1 hour in preheated 350-degree oven.

Makes 6 servings.

DUCK AND WILD RICE CASSEROLE

Representative **Tommy Robinson**—*Arkansas*
Recipe from: Carolyn Robinson

This dish is a favorite of many Arkansans, especially during duck season. If you don't have ducks, try substituting chicken—it's still good.

2 medium-sized ducks (about 3 cups cubed meat)
3 stalks celery
1 medium-sized onion, halved
  Salt to taste
  Black pepper to taste
1 6-ounce package seasoned wild and long-grained rice
½ cup margarine
½ cup chopped onion
¼ cup all-purpose white flour
1 4-ounce can sliced mushrooms
1½ cups half-and-half
1 tablespoon chopped fresh parsley
1 teaspoon salt
¼ teaspoon black pepper
  Slivered almonds

Simmer ducks for 1 hour (or until tender) in water to cover, along with celery, onion halves, salt and pepper. Remove ducks from liquid, cool and cube meat; reserve broth. Cook rice according to package directions.

Melt margarine and sauté chopped onion; stir in flour until well blended and smooth. Drain mushrooms, reserving liquid. Add mushrooms to onion mixture. Add enough duck broth to mushroom liquid to make 1½ cups broth; stir this into onion mixture. Add all remaining ingredients except almonds, mixing well. Pour into greased 2-quart casserole. Sprinkle almonds on top.

Bake, covered, in preheated 350-degree oven for 20 to 25 minutes. Uncover and bake for 5 to 10 minutes until very hot. (This casserole can be prepared ahead of time and refrigerated.)

Makes 6 servings.

EASY BUT RICH BEEF CASSEROLE

Representative **John D. Dingell**—*Michigan*
Recipe from: Debbie Dingell

1½ **pounds stewing beef, trimmed and cut into 2-inch pieces**
½ **cup red dinner wine**
1 **10½-ounce can undiluted beef consommé**
1 **4-ounce can mushrooms, drained**
  Salt to taste
  Black pepper to taste
1 **medium-sized onion, peeled and sliced**
¼ **cup bread crumbs**
¼ **cup all-purpose white flour**

Combine beef, wine, consommé, mushrooms, salt, pepper, and onion in casserole dish. Mix bread crumbs with flour and stir into mixture.

Cover and bake in preheated 300-degree oven for about 3 hours or until beef is tender.

SHEPHERD'S PIE (ENGLISH BEEF AND POTATO CASSEROLE)

Senator **Bob Packwood**—*Oregon*

¼ pound ground beef *per person*
1 small onion *per person,* chopped
2 potatoes *per person,* peeled and
   freshly cooked
Cream
Salt to taste
Black pepper to taste
Ground nutmeg to taste
Lots of grated Cheddar cheese, for
   garnish
Lumps of butter
Paprika for garnish

Sauté ground beef and chopped onions together.
Drain and layer in bottom of casserole. Mash potatoes
with enough cream to yield soft, fluffy consistency;
season with salt, pepper and nutmeg. Layer potatoes
on top of beef and onions. Sprinkle top with grated
cheese. Dot top with lumps of butter. Sprinkle top
with paprika. Bake for 30 minutes in preheated
350-degree oven.

PORK CHOPS AND SPANISH RICE

Representative **Henry B. Gonzalez**—*Texas*

4 **pork chops, seasoned with salt and pepper**
2 **tablespoons vegetable oil**
1 **cup uncooked white rice (or brown rice)**
1 **medium-sized onion, chopped**
¼ **cup chopped green pepper**
1 **jalapeño or serrano pepper, chopped (optional)**
3 **ounces tomato sauce**
Garlic salt to taste
Cayenne pepper to taste
Black pepper to taste
Boiling water to cook rice

In heavy skillet, brown pork chops, and set aside. In second (or cleaned skillet, if same skillet is used) pour oil. Heat over medium heat, and add rice. Stir rice until it loses its translucency and puffs (but not until it turns brown, although a few pieces may brown). Stir in onion and peppers. Stir together tomato sauce, garlic salt, cayenne and black pepper. Stir mixture into onion and peppers. Lay pork chops on top of rice mixture, add enough boiling water to cook rice and cover. Cook until the water has been absorbed, and the rice is tender. Add more boiling water, if necessary, to prevent pan from boiling dry.

Variation: Chicken and Spanish Rice—Pieces of chicken may be boiled gently for about 15 minutes and then laid on rice before it is cooked. Finish cooking chicken with rice, at a low-medium heat, adding boiling cooking liquid from chicken.

Variation: Ground Meat and Spanish Rice—Brown in skillet 1 pound of ground meat with onion, peppers, and seasoning to taste. Add meat mixture to rice just before it is completely done and all water is absorbed.

PORK CHOPS AND BROWN RICE CASSEROLE

Representative **John Seiberling**—*Ohio*

This is an easy casserole, all done ahead of time. If an ovenproof and stove-top casserole is used, just one utensil is needed for the whole process. We often have a green salad with it. It is always good and a favorite of the Seiberling family.

3 tablespoons green onions, chopped
3 tablespoons green pepper, chopped
2 tablespoons vegetable oil
4 to 6 pork chops
1 16-ounce can tomatoes (or 2 cups fresh tomatoes, cut up)
1 cup uncooked brown rice
1 cup beef bouillon
Salt to taste
Black pepper to taste

Cook onion and green pepper slowly in oil for 4 to 5 minutes. Remove from skillet and reserve. Brown pork chops on both sides. Place in casserole; add tomatoes, rice and bouillon to cover; add green pepper and onions, salt and pepper. Bake in preheated 350-degree oven for 1 to 1½ hours or until meat and rice are tender.

Makes 4 to 6 servings.

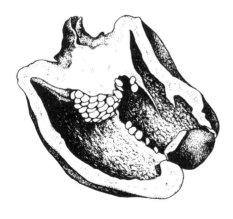

CHALUPA CASSEROLE

Representative **Eldon Rudd**—*Arizona*

1 4- to 5-pound fresh pork roast
2 large cans chili beans or small red
   beans
1 can green chili sauce (salsa)
   Garlic salt to taste
2 tablespoons chili powder
1 tablespoon ground cumin
1 teaspoon dried oregano leaves
2 teaspoons salt, or to taste
1 4-ounce can chopped green chilies

To serve:

Corn chips
Shredded lettuce
Grated cheese
Tabasco sauce
Sour cream
Chopped onion (optional)
Diced tomato (optional)
Diced avocado (optional)

Cook pork roast covered in water until cooked through. Remove meat from bone and break up into pieces. Place in large pot; add beans with liquid and remaining ingredients. Mix thoroughly. Cook on low heat for 45 minutes. Add water if too thick. Pour over corn chips and top with lettuce, cheese, hot sauce, sour cream and optional toppings, if desired.

Serves 10.

HAM AND HOMINY

Representative **Pat Roberts**—*Kansas*

The following recipe was handed down from my husband's family. According to his mother, Mrs. Ruth Roberts, when one relative came for dinner, he always asked for Hog and Hominy. He was a Kansan but not a farmer.
—Franki Roberts

1 **3-inch-thick slice cured ham**
Prepared mustard
Brown sugar
1 to 2 **cans hominy, drained**
Milk

Brush both sides of ham with a mixture of mustard and brown sugar. A little extra may be put on top. Pour hominy around ham. Add enough milk to pan to cover hominy. Cover and bake in preheated 300-degree oven for 2½ hours; uncover and bake 30 minutes longer.

SAUSAGE SOUFFLÉ

Senator **Paul Simon**—*Illinois*

This recipe is splendid for a brunch; preparation should be done the night before.

6 **slices white bread (crusts removed), cut into cubes**
1 **pound bulk pork sausage, browned and drained**
8 **eggs**
1 **teaspoon salt**
1 **teaspoon dry mustard**
2 **cups milk**
1 **cup shredded mild Cheddar cheese**

Grease 9 x 13-inch flat casserole. Arrange layer of bread, then sausage. Beat together eggs, salt, mustard, and milk. Pour mixture over bread. Top with cheese and cover with plastic wrap. Refrigerate overnight. Bake at 350 degrees for 45 minutes.

Makes 8 servings.

SAUSAGE CASSEROLE

Representative **Bob McEwen**—*Ohio*

1 **bunch celery, including leaves**
½ **cup uncooked white rice**
2 **packages Lipton onion soup mix**
1 **pound bulk sausage**
1 **medium-sized onion, chopped**
5 **cups boiling water**

Chop celery stalks into ½-inch pieces. Combine with rice and soup mix and place into 9 x 13-inch flat baking dish. Brown sausage and onion. Drain well and stir into mixture. Add 5 cups of boiling water. Cook, covered, in a preheated 325-degree oven for 2 to 3 hours.

LYNN'S LASAGNA

Representative **Lynn Martin**—*Illinois*

> 1½ **pounds ground beef**
> 3 to 4 **15-ounce cans tomato sauce**
> 3 **6-ounce cans tomato paste**
> ⅓ **cup water**
> 2 **tablespoons dried parsley flakes, divided**
> 1 **teaspoon salt, divided**
> 1 **teaspoon dried basil leaves, divided**
> ½ **teaspoon dried oregano leaves**
> ½ **teaspoon granulated sugar**
> 1 **pound mozzarella cheese, shredded**
> 1 **pound creamed cottage cheese**
> 1 **egg, slightly beaten**
> **Black pepper to taste**
> 9 **lasagna noodles, cooked**
> **Grated Parmesan cheese**

Brown beef; drain excess fat. Add tomato sauce, tomato paste, water, 1 tablespoon parsley flakes, and ½ teaspoon *each* salt, basil, oregano, and sugar. Simmer for 25 minutes.

Stir together ¼ of mozzarella, the cottage cheese, egg, and remaining parsley, basil and salt. Put one-fourth of sauce in bottom of 9 x 13-inch oblong baking dish. Lay 3 cooked lasagna noodles over sauce. Then top with one-third of cottage cheese mixture and one-third of remaining mozzarella. Sprinkle with Parmesan cheese. Repeat sequence twice, ending with a layer of sauce on top.

Bake in a 350-degree oven for 45 minutes to 1 hour, or until bubbly. This dish freezes well and can be frozen prior to final cooking.

Makes 8 to 10 servings.

BAKED LASAGNA WITH ITALIAN SAUCE

Representative **Romano L. Mazzoli**—*Kentucky*
Recipe from: Mrs. Mazzoli

Sauce
- 1 pound lean ground beef
- 1 medium-sized onion, minced
- 4 6-ounce cans tomato paste
- 9 tomato paste cans water
- 1 4-ounce can mushrooms, drained and chopped
- ½ teaspoon minced fresh garlic
- ½ teaspoon red pepper
- 1 teaspoon dried basil leaves
- ½ teaspoon granulated sugar
- Salt to taste

Other ingredients
- 1 pound lasagna noodles
- 2 tablespoons salt
- 1 tablespoon oil
- ½ cup grated romano cheese
- 12 meatballs (optional)

To prepare sauce, brown ground beef and onions. Add tomato paste and water and mix well. Add all other sauce ingredients and bring to a full boil. Reduce heat and simmer at least 3 hours, stirring occasionally.

Cook lasagna noodles in very large pot of water as directed on package, adding salt and oil to the boiling water. Spread some meat sauce lightly over bottom of greased 9 x 13-inch casserole. Cover with a layer of noodles, spread a thin covering of sauce over them and sprinkle with cheese. Repeat layers in the order given until all noodles and sauce are used, ending with cheese. If desired, place meatballs evenly spaced on top of noodles.

Cover with heavy aluminum foil and bake at 250 degrees for 40 minutes. Cut into 4-inch squares and spoon sauce over top of each. May be frozen and then baked for 1 hour at 200 degrees, then 40 minutes at 250 degrees.

Makes 8 servings.

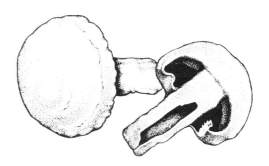

ITALIAN MEAT PIE

Representative **Joseph P. Addabbo**—*New York*

2 **packages pizza dough**
Black pepper to taste
Salt to taste
¼ **pound sliced ham**
¼ **pound sliced provolone cheese**
¼ **pound sliced Genoa salami**
1 **8-ounce can tomato sauce**

Roll out one package pizza dough. Season with salt and pepper. Top with layers of ham, cheese, and salami. Spread tomato sauce on top. Roll out second package of pizza dough and place on top of layered meats. Pinch sides of crusts together firmly.

Place on greased baking pan. Bake for 40 minutes in preheated 325-degree oven.

HOUSTON MEAT AND CHEESE PIE

Representative **Tom DeLay**—*Texas*

½ **pound ground beef**
½ **cup mayonnaise**
½ **cup milk**
2 **eggs**
2 **tablespoons all-purpose white flour**
¾ **cup grated Cheddar cheese**
¾ **cup grated Swiss cheese**
⅓ **cup sliced green onions**
   Salt to taste
   Black pepper to taste
1 **9-inch unbaked pastry shell**

Brown meat in a medium skillet; drain and set aside.
Blend mayonnaise, milk, eggs and flour until smooth.
Stir in meat, cheese, onion, salt and pepper. Turn
mixture into unbaked pastry shell. Bake at 350
degrees for 35 to 40 minutes. This freezes well if
there is any left over.

Makes 4 to 6 servings.

MIKE'S FAVORITE CHICKEN PIE

Representative **Mike DeWine**—*Ohio*

My wife can attest to the fact that the following recipe would be my favorite!

1 **4- to 5-pound chicken**
1 **medium-sized onion**
1 **stalk celery**
1 **recipe pastry for a single-crust pie**
Sauce
6 **tablespoons butter or chicken fat**
6 **tablespoons all-purpose white flour**
2¼ **cups chicken broth**
1 **12-ounce can evaporated milk**
Salt to taste
Black pepper to taste

Stew chicken with onion and celery in water until tender; cool. Bone chicken and cut into bite-sized pieces (2 to 3 cups meat). Separate fat and broth; reserve.

To prepare crust, roll out 1 recipe of your favorite pastry ¼-inch thick. Cut out shape to fit top of casserole to be used. Prick crust and bake on baking sheet in preheated 375-degree oven until golden.

Meanwhile, prepare sauce: Stir together butter and flour in saucepan until well blended and smooth. Gradually add chicken broth and milk, stirring. Season with salt and pepper. Heat, stirring, until slightly thickened. Stir chicken into sauce. Pour into casserole. Bake in preheated 375-degree oven until bubbling. Top with prebaked crust when ready to serve.

Main Dishes

BUTTE PASTY

Representative **Pat Williams**—*Montana*
Recipe from: *Butte Heritage Cookbook*

Pasty is pronounced "pas-tee." Old-timers claim the pasty arrived in Butte, Montana along with the first housewives who followed their husbands into the mining camp. Long favored in the copper miner's lunch bucket, the pastry-wrapped meal of meat and vegetables was an ideal way for "Cousin Jeanie" to provide a hearty meal for hard-working "Cousin Jack." As the miner unwrapped his lunch, he would fondly refer to the pasty as a "letter from 'ome." Its popularity spread quickly throughout the camp, and today the pasty is as much a part of Butte as the Berkeley Pit.

Pastry
   3 cups all-purpose white flour
   ½ to 1 teaspoon salt, or to taste
   1¼ cups lard or shortening
   ¾ cup very cold water
Filling
   5 or 6 medium-sized potatoes (red are best), sliced
   3 medium-sized or 2 large yellow onions, sliced
   Fresh or dried chopped parsley, to taste
   2 pounds beef loin tip, skirting or flank steak, sliced into thin strips
   Butter
   Salt to taste
   Black pepper to taste
   Milk

Measure flour and salt into a bowl. Cut in lard until dough resembles small peas. Add water and form dough. Divide into 6 equal parts.

Roll each dough portion out, slightly oblong, about ¼ to ⅓ inch thick. Arrange in layers on dough first potatoes, then onions and parsley, then meat. Dot with butter and season with salt and pepper. Bring pasty dough up from ends and crimp across top. (Making the pasty oblong eliminates lump of dough on each end.) Bake in preheated 375-degree oven for about 1 hour. Brush a little milk on top while baking.

Makes 6 pasties.

COPPER COUNTRY PASTIES

Representative **Robert W. Davis**—*Michigan*

My congressional district represents the northern 40 percent of the Great Lake State, Michigan. Though representing an area of approximately 23,000 square miles, I have been fortunate to learn much about our rich heritage. We have many Polish, Italian, Swedish, Finnish and Native American descendants. This recipe comes from the early Finnish and Cornish miners that worked in the copper and iron ore mines. Enjoy your pasties.

Dough

- 3 **cups all-purpose white flour**
- 1½ **sticks butter (cold and cut into bits)**
- 1½ **teaspoons salt**
- 6 **tablespoons cold water**

Filling

- 1 **pound round steak, cut into ½-inch cubes**
- 1 **pound boneless pork loin, cut into ½-inch cubes**
- 5 **carrots, chopped**
- 2 **large onions, chopped**
- 2 **potatoes, peeled and chopped**
- ½ **rutabaga, peeled and chopped**
- 2 **teaspoons salt**
- ½ **teaspoon black pepper**

Other ingredients

- 6 **teaspoons butter**
- **Ketchup**

In a large bowl, combine flour, butter and salt. Blend ingredients until well combined and add water, one tablespoon at a time, to form dough. Toss mixture until it forms a ball. Knead dough lightly against a smooth surface with heel of hand to distribute fat evenly. Form into a ball and dust with flour. Wrap in wax paper and chill for 30 minutes.

Combine all filling ingredients in large bowl and stir to mix. Divide dough into 6 pieces and roll one piece into a 10-inch round on a lightly floured surface. Put 1½ cups filling on one-half of the round. Moisten edges and fold unfilled half over filling to enclose it. Pinch edges together to seal and crimp with fork. Transfer pasty to lightly buttered baking sheet and cut several slits in top. Roll out and fill remaining dough portions.

Bake in preheated 350-degree oven for 30 minutes. Put teaspoon of butter on each pasty and bake for 30 minutes longer. Remove, cover with damp towel and cool for 15 minutes. Serve with ketchup.

Makes 6 pasties.

SPICY ITALIAN SANDWICHES

Representative **Bruce Vento**—*Minnesota*

This recipe is an old favorite of the Vento family and is served often.

2½ cups bread crumbs
¼ cup romano cheese
2 small garlic cloves, minced
1 tablespoon dry (hot) red pepper flakes
1½ teaspoons dried parsley leaves
1½ teaspoons dried basil leaves
1 teaspoon black pepper
Salt to taste
2 large eggs
Milk
4 pounds ground beef
Olive oil for cooking

Sauce
1 42-ounce can tomato juice
1 16-ounce can tomato puree
1 6-ounce can tomato paste

To serve:
Italian bread

Mix together bread crumbs, cheese, garlic, red pepper flakes, parsley, basil, pepper, salt and eggs. Add milk until mixture is consistency of moist dressing. Add ground beef to mixture and combine thoroughly, preferably with your hands. Shape into patties. Fry patties in olive oil only until browned. (These burn easily so watch carefully and keep adding oil.) After browning, place patties in a large greased Dutch oven. Stir together sauce ingredients and add to Dutch oven.

Simmer patties in sauce over low heat for about 1 hour. Watch carefully as patties tend to stick to bottom of pan. Serve patties on Italian bread.

SENATOR'S MIDNIGHT SUPPER

Senator **Richard G. Lugar**—*Indiana*

This is the sort of thing Dick likes when he gets home late at night from meetings or speaking engagements. I can put it together in a hurry, and most of the ingredients are always on hand on the pantry shelf. The dish is also good for brunch.
—Char Lugar

2 slices toast
3 eggs
2 tablespoons sour cream, or imitation sour cream
Salt to taste
Butter for cooking
1 can asparagus spears
½ 10-ounce can Cheddar cheese soup (undiluted)
Paprika for garnish

Trim crusts from toast. Lightly beat together eggs, sour cream and salt with a fork. Then melt butter in skillet and scramble egg mixture. In separate pan, heat asparagus. In third pan, heat cheese soup. Place hot drained asparagus spears on toast. Top with scrambled eggs. Serve with sausage, bacon or Canadian bacon and a green salad.

Serves 2.

Chapter 6

Meats

Beef

Pork

Ham

Lamb

Veal

LITE AND LEAN BEEF BROIL

Representative **Larry Craig**—*Idaho*

Four ounces of cooked beef provide 325 calories, at least 50% of your daily protein requirement, at least 20% of your daily iron requirement and over 50% of your daily need for vitamin B-12.

½ cup soy sauce
¼ cup water
2 tablespoons lemon juice
2 tablespoons (1-ounce) honey
1 teaspoon instant minced onions
¼ teaspoon garlic powder
1½ pounds beef sirloin steak, top round, flank or brisket

Combine all ingredients except beef in a noncorrosive pan. Add beef and turn to coat. Cover and marinate beef for 24 to 48 hours in refrigerator.

Broil beef to desired doneness (do not overcook; best served medium rare). To serve, slice beef across the grain into thin slices.

Makes 4 to 6 servings.

BEEF PEPPER STEAK

Senator **Ed Zorinsky**—*Nebraska*

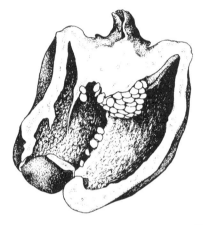

3 pounds beef tenderloin (sliced thin and cut into 2-inch squares)
¼ cup butter, divided
1 teaspoon dried oregano leaves
Salt to taste
Garlic salt to taste
Freshly ground black pepper to taste
1 pound fresh mushrooms
3 green peppers, cut into 1-inch squares
3 tomatoes, quartered
¼ cup tomato paste
¼ cup sherry

Brown meat in 2 tablespoons butter. Add seasonings and continue cooking until tender (about 15 minutes). In another pan, sauté mushrooms and green pepper in remaining butter for 5 minutes. Add to meat mixture along with tomatoes, tomato paste and sherry. Heat through and serve at once.

Makes about 8 servings.

ROUND STEAK

Representative **Webb Franklin**—*Mississippi*

Representative Webb Franklin describes his dish as "an epicurean delight . . . guaranteed to 'juke' your hunger pains."

1 large, 3-inch-thick top round steak
  (6 to 10 pounds)
Meat tenderizer
Garlic salt
Lemon-pepper seasoning
Black pepper to taste
1 stick butter

Take a big fork and juke (poke) holes all over meat. Then shake meat tenderizer, garlic salt, lemon-pepper seasoning, and black pepper all over meat. Let meat remain, uncovered, for at least 4 hours at room temperature (the longer, the better).*

Start charcoal fire and get it as hot as you can. When fire is at its hottest, put meat on grill. Sear all sides, then cook for about 20 minutes, turning only twice. (You will think it's burning, but don't worry, it's supposed to.)

Remove from fire and put meat on well and tree cutting board on top of stick of butter. Slice meat thinly and use juice from meat mixed with butter for gravy. The end product should look and taste like tenderloin. (Done around the outside and red in the middle.)

Editor's note: Most cooks may prefer to follow standard kitchen practice and cover and refrigerate meat during marinating period.

Makes 10 servings.

BEEF SUKIYAKI

Senator **Spark M. Matsunaga**—*Hawaii*

1 large onion, sliced
6 mushrooms, sliced
Beef suet
1 6½-ounce can bamboo shoots, drained and sliced
1 package yam noodles
¼ cup mirin (rice wine)
½ cup soy sauce
¼ cup water
⅓ cup granulated sugar
1 block tofu, cubed
2 won bok leaves, cut in 1-inch pieces
1 pound beef steak (New York cut), thinly sliced
2 scallions, cut in 1-inch pieces

In a large skillet, sauté onions and mushrooms in suet. Add bamboo shoots, yam noodles and mirin until well mixed. Combine soy sauce, water and sugar and add to mixture, cooking until it bubbles. Add tofu, won bok, beef and scallions, turning beef as it cooks. Tofu must be handled gently or it will not retain its shape. Do not overcook beef.

Makes 6 servings.

THAD COCHRAN'S FAVORITE MEAT LOAF

Senator **Thad Cochran**—*Mississippi*

1½ **pounds ground beef**
1 **cup cracker crumbs**
2 **eggs, beaten**
1 **8-ounce can tomato sauce (with tomato bits)**
½ **cup finely chopped onion**
2 **tablespoons chopped green pepper**
1 **medium-sized bay leaf, crushed**
  Pinch dried thyme leaves
  Pinch dried marjoram leaves

Preheat oven to 350 degrees. Mix ingredients thoroughly. Place in lightly greased loaf pan. Bake for 1 hour.

MADRAS MEATLOAF

Representative **Denny Smith**—*Oregon*

- 2 **pounds ground beef**
- 1 **medium-sized onion**
- ¼ **cup cracker crumbs**
- ¾ **cup fruit chutney**
- 1 **5-ounce can cream of celery soup**
- 1 **teaspoon curry powder**
- ½ **teaspoon ground ginger**
- ½ **teaspoon dried basil leaves**
- ¼ **teaspoon ground mace**
- **Salt to taste**
- **Black pepper to taste**

Mix ingredients in order given. Shape into loaf in shallow pan. Bake in preheated 350-degree oven for 1 hour.

Makes 6 servings.

MARTIN'S DUTCH OVEN MEATLOAF

Representative **Lynn Martin**—*Illinois*

When left over, this also happens to make the best cold sandwiches in the world.

1 **pound meatloaf mix***
Salt to taste
Black pepper to taste
1 **large onion (or 2 small ones), chopped**
2 **slices bread, diced or torn into small pieces**
½ **green pepper, very thinly sliced**
1 **16-ounce can whole tomatoes**
1 **1-pound bag carrots, peeled and cut into thirds**
2 to 2½ **tablespoons all-purpose white flour**
Cold water
Milk
To serve:
Mashed potatoes

In a large bowl, mix meatloaf mix, salt and pepper, onion, bread and green pepper. Add drained tomatoes; reserve juice. Mix this all together, adding just a little of reserved juice if necessary. Put mixture in Dutch oven in a rounded mound. Lay carrots around meatloaf. Bake, covered, in preheated 350-degree oven for 1 hour 45 minutes to 2 hours; the last 30 minutes, remove lid so meatloaf will brown. Make sure there is liquid in bottom of Dutch oven to prevent burning; use leftover juice from tomatoes.

Meats

When meatloaf is done, put on plate surrounded by carrots. Loaf will be very soft so you usually have to cut it in half. Leave a huge chunk of meatloaf in pot. Transfer Dutch oven to stove top. Stir small amount of water together with flour until smooth. Stir into pot, crumbling meatloaf chunk. Add milk to form a gravy. Serve along with meatloaf, carrots and mashed potatoes.

Note: Meatloaf mix is available at most supermarkets. Generally, it's 3 parts ground beef and 1 part ground pork and veal.

SWEDISH MEATBALLS

Representative **Charles W. Stenholm**—*Texas*

This is an old family favorite from the Stenholm household.

1¼ **pounds ground beef**
¼ **pound ground pork**
1½ **cups soft bread crumbs (about 3 slices bread)**
1 **cup light cream or half-and-half**
½ **cup chopped onion**
3 **tablespoons butter or margarine, divided**
1 **egg**
¼ **teaspoon ground ginger**
Dash ground nutmeg
Salt to taste
Black pepper to taste
3 **tablespoons all-purpose white flour**
¾ **cup canned condensed beef broth (do not dilute)**
¼ **cup water**
¼ **teaspoon instant coffee**

Mix meats together. Soak bread crumbs in cream about 5 minutes. Cook onion in 1 tablespoon butter until tender. Combine meat, crumb mixture, egg, onion and seasonings. Beat vigorously with electric mixer until fluffy. Form in 1½-inch balls. (Mixture will be soft.)

Brown meatballs in remaining 2 tablespoons butter, shaking skillet to keep balls round. Remove meatballs. Stir flour into drippings in skillet; add broth, water, and coffee. Heat and stir until gravy thickens. Return meatballs to gravy. Cover and cook slowly about 30 minutes, basting occasionally. May be frozen.

Makes about 3 dozen.

MEATBALLS POMPA ITALIANO

Representative **Douglas Applegate**—*Ohio*

The grandmother of an old friend of mine brought this recipe from Italy and it is delectable.
—Douglas Applegate

1 **pound ground chuck**
¼ **pound Italian sausage**
2 **eggs**
1 **tablespoon chopped fresh parsley**
1 or 2 **garlic cloves, crushed or finely chopped**
Salt to taste
Black pepper to taste
1 **slice white bread**
Milk
1 **small onion, chopped**
Vegetable oil
¼ **medium-sized green pepper, chopped**

Mix together chuck, sausage and eggs. Add parsley, garlic, salt and pepper and mix. Soak bread in milk. Then squeeze out excess milk from bread and blend bread into meat mixture. Roll mixture into meatballs (whatever size you desire).

Sauté onion in a small amount of oil. Add green pepper. Add ½ to 1 inch of oil. Heat oil, add meatballs and sauté until browned. Add meatballs to your favorite spaghetti sauce and cook until sauce is done.

Makes 6 to 8 servings.

SHERRY'S SPAGHETTI SAUCE WITH MEATBALLS

Representative **Sherwood Boehlert**—*New York*

Sauce
- 1½ pounds Italian sausage
- 1 28-ounce can tomato puree
- ½ can water
- 1 6-ounce can tomato paste
- 1 to 2 teaspoons granulated sugar
- 2 teaspoons dried oregano leaves
- 2 bay leaves
- 1 teaspoon salt
- 2 garlic cloves, chopped
- 3 tablespoons oil (reserved from meatballs)
- 3 teaspoons dried basil leaves

Meatballs
- 1 pound ground beef
- ½ cup bread crumbs
- 2 eggs
- 2 tablespoons romano cheese
- 1 teaspoon salt
- 1 teaspoon pepper
- Garlic salt to taste
- 1 tablespoon parsley flakes

Fry sausage in large skillet until brown. Mix all remaining sauce ingredients, except sausage, in large pot. Add sausage; reserve fat in skillet. Mix all ingredients for meatballs. Shape into meatballs and brown in about 4 to 5 tablespoons of reserved fat from sausage, turning frequently. Add browned meatballs to sauce and simmer for at least 3 hours.

ITALIAN SPAGHETTI SAUCE

Senator **James Abdnor**—*South Dakota*
Recipe from: Mary Wehby Abdnor
(Senator Abdnor's mother)

½ cup chopped onion
2 tablespoons olive or vegetable oil
1 pound ground beef
1 clove garlic, minced
2 16-ounce cans tomatoes, including juice
2 8-ounce cans seasoned tomato sauce
1 3-ounce can broiled sliced mushrooms (optional)
1 teaspoon dried oregano leaves
½ teaspoon dried, crumbled sage leaves
1 teaspoon salt
Dash black pepper
1 bay leaf
1 cup water

To serve:
Hot cooked spaghetti
Grated Parmesan cheese

In a large skillet, cook onion in hot oil until almost tender. Add ground beef and garlic; brown lightly. Add all remaining ingredients; simmer, uncovered, stirring occasionally for 2 hours or until thick. Remove bay leaf.

Serve sauce over hot cooked spaghetti. Pass bowl of grated Parmesan cheese.

Makes 6 servings.

PORCUPINES

Representative **John Kasich**—*Ohio*

> 1 **pound ground beef**
> 1 **tablespoon finely minced onions**
> 2 **teaspoons baking powder**
>   **Salt to taste**
>   **Black pepper to taste**
> ½ **cup uncooked white rice**
> ¾ **cup milk**
> 1 **8-ounce can tomato sauce**

Combine all ingredients except tomato sauce. After mixing well, form into 8 or 9 round balls. Pour tomato sauce over all and bake in an uncovered pan in preheated 400-degree oven for 35 minutes. Cover and cook for 35 minutes more.

SENATOR BYRD'S FAVORITE CABBAGE ROLLS

Senator **Robert C. Byrd**—*West Virginia*
Recipe from: Mrs. Byrd

1 pound lean ground beef
1 cup cooked white rice
1 small onion, chopped
1 teaspoon salt
¼ teaspoon black pepper
1 egg
　Cabbage leaves
　Vegetable oil
2 8-ounce cans tomato sauce
¼ cup water

Mix ground beef, cooked rice, chopped onion, salt, pepper and egg together. Trim off thickest part of stem from cabbage leaves. Divide meat into equal portions, wrap each in a leaf, fasten with wooden picks. Brown cabbage rolls slightly in oil. Add tomato sauce and water to pan. Cover and cook slowly for about 40 minutes.

STUFFED CABBAGE ROLLS

Senator **James Abdnor**—*South Dakota*
Recipe from: Mary Wehby Abdnor
(Senator Abdnor's mother)

> 1 head cabbage (about 2 pounds)
> 1 pound meat (lamb or beef, ground or cut into ½-inch or smaller cubes)
> 1 cup uncooked white rice, soaked in cold water and drained
> ½ teaspoon ground cinnamon
> ½ teaspoon salt
> Black pepper to taste
> 3 tablespoons melted butter
> 1 16-ounce can whole tomatoes, including juice
> Water
> Juice of ½ lemon

Core cabbage and insert whole head in boiling water to wilt leaves. Drain and separate leaves. Mix together meat and rice. Add cinnamon, salt, pepper, and melted butter. For each roll, put about 1 tablespoon meat and rice mixture in half a cabbage leaf.

Line saucepan with 2 or 3 cabbage leaves. Add cabbage rolls, arranging them evenly. Add tomatoes and enough water to cover rolls completely. Add lemon juice. Bring to boil; lower heat to medium and cook, covered, for about 45 minutes, or until rice is tender.

MOTHER DYSON'S MARYLAND STUFFED HAM

Representative **Roy Dyson**—*Maryland*
Recipe from: Marie Dyson

> 1 **pound kale, coarse stems and ribs removed**
> 6 **pounds cabbage**
> 3 **pounds onions**
>   **About 2 tablespoons celery seeds**
>   **Salt to taste**
>   **Black pepper to taste**
>   **Red pepper to taste**
> 1 **12-pound corned ham or country cured ham**

Chop, then blanch kale. Chop cabbage and onions in small pieces (if you can stand the tears from onions). Mix all vegetables together and add all seasonings.

To get ham ready for stuffing, cut deep slits down length of ham. Pack and push as much stuffing mixture into slits as possible, covering top of ham if any is left over. Put into clean cheesecloth bag. (Or use a pillowcase. It's easier to just tie at top and there's not much chance of stuffing falling out.)

Cook in large pot at least 4 hours; start timing when water begins to boil and keep boiling entire time. Place a rack (I use an aluminum pie tin) in bottom of pan, to prevent ham from sticking to bottom. Cool before slicing.

Note: Pot liquid used to cook ham is excellent for seasoning vegetables.

MT. VERNON HAM IN RED WINE

Senator **Mark O. Hatfield**—*Oregon*

          10 to 11 pound ham, rinsed in cold water
                4 onions, each studded with 2 cloves
                1 tablespoon whole black peppercorns
                ¼ teaspoon ground mace
                   Bouquet garni (6 sprigs parsley,
                      ½ teaspoon dried thyme leaves,
                      2 bay leaves)
     Basting sauce
                6 tablespoons butter
                3 tablespoons all-purpose white flour
                3 tablespoons packed dark brown
                   sugar
                3 cups dry red wine
                1 cup beef broth
Crumb mixture
                1½ cups dry bread crumbs
                ⅓ cup dark brown sugar, packed
                ¼ teaspoon ground cloves
                ¼ teaspoon salt
Serving sauce
                ¼ cup currant jelly
                ¼ cup dry red wine
                ¼ cup beef broth

In large pot cover ham with 1 inch water. Bring ham, onions and seasoning ingredients just to boiling point; reduce heat and gently simmer, partly covered, for 2½ hours. Let cool in broth. Using sharp knife, remove ham skin and fat, leaving ¼ inch layer of fat. Put ham in roasting pan.

To prepare basting sauce, melt butter in a saucepan. Stir in flour, then sugar. Cook until sugar has dissolved. Remove from heat and stir in wine and beef broth. Bring sauce to a boil. Pour sauce over ham and bake in preheated 400-degree oven for 30 minutes, basting often. (When ham is done, reserve basting sauce.)

To prepare crumb mixture, in a bowl combine bread crumbs, sugar, cloves and salt. Spoon this mixture over fat side of ham, pressing it on with back side of spoon. Moisten crumb mix with basting sauce and bake for 30 minutes more or until brown. (Cover crust with foil if it gets too brown.) Transfer ham to separate dish; reserve basting sauce.

To prepare serving sauce, add jelly, wine and beef broth to reserved basting sauce. Cook till jelly dissolves. Strain and pour into sauce boat and serve with ham.

MARY'S TENNESSEE COUNTRY HAM

Senator **Jim Sasser**—*Tennessee*

This recipe is a favorite of many Tennesseans, particularly around the Thanksgiving and Christmas holiday seasons. I trust that this favorite of mine will become a favorite of yours.

1 **large country ham**
  Bread crumbs
  Apple cider
  Brown sugar

Put ham in lard stand (or very large pot) and totally cover with water. Boil 1½ minutes per pound. Place top on lard stand and remove from stove. Wrap stand in old newspapers, old blanket or any other heavy fabric that will hold heat. Allow ham to remain wrapped up for 20 to 22 hours.

Skin ham. When cool, take to your butcher. Ask him to debone it and grind all lean scraps from the trimming and deboning. Then, combine equal parts of ground ham, bread crumbs, apple cider and brown sugar. This makes a stuffing to go back into cavity left by boning. (Stuffing should be consistency of turkey stuffing.) Put stuffed ham in preheated 300-degree oven and bake for 30 to 40 minutes.

PHILIP CRANE'S FAVORITE HAM LOAF

Representative **Philip M. Crane**—*Illinois*

>   2 **pounds ground ham**
>   1 **pound ground fresh pork**
>   2 **eggs**
>   1½ **cups cracker crumbs**
>   1 **cup milk**
>   **Garlic salt to taste**
> **Topping and garnish**
>   1½ **cups brown sugar, packed**
>   1½ **teaspoons dry mustard**
>   1 **10½-ounce can tomato soup**
>   **Raisins and/or pineapple for garnish**

Mix all ham loaf ingredients together well. Shape into loaf in pan. To prepare topping, mix together sugar, mustard and soup. Pour over loaf. Garnish with raisins and/or pineapple, if desired. Bake ham loaf in preheated 350-degree oven for 1½ hours.

ANNIE GLENN'S HAM LOAF

Senator **John Glenn**—*Ohio*
Recipe from: Annie Glenn

     1 **pound cured ham, ground**
     ½ **pound fresh ham, ground**
     1½ **cups dry bread crumbs**
     2 **eggs, beaten**
     ¾ **cup milk**
        Black pepper to taste
  Dressing
     ¼ **cup granulated sugar**
     ¼ **cup apple cider vinegar**
     ½ **cup water**
     1 **tablespoon prepared mustard**

Mix ham loaf ingredients together well. Form into
loaf in loaf pan. To prepare dressing, dissolve sugar
in water and vinegar; add mustard. Pour ¾ of
dressing over loaf; baste frequently (dressing will be
syrupy). Add additional dressing, if necessary. Bake
in preheated 350-degree oven for 1½ hours.

Makes 4 to 6 servings.

BRATS 'N KRAUT

Senator **Bob Kasten**—*Wisconsin*

This is typical Wisconsin fare and should be served on hard rolls with potato salad as a side dish.

1½ **pounds sauerkraut**
1 **teaspoon caraway seeds**
2 **tablespoons brown sugar, packed**
8 **bratwurst sausages**
2 **12-ounce cans beer**

Mix sauerkraut, caraway seeds and sugar together. Let simmer gently. Meanwhile, boil bratwurst in beer until almost ready to burst. Remove from beer and brown on a hot grill or griddle. Add leftover beer broth to sauerkraut to taste.

Makes 8 servings.

SWEET AND SOUR PORK

Senator **E. J. (Jake) Garn**—*Utah*

This became one of my favorite recipes during my time in Japan.

Sauce
- 1½ teaspoons cornstarch
- 2 teaspoons water
- ¼ cup apple cider vinegar
- 1 teaspoon soy sauce
- ½ cup brown sugar, packed
- 1 cup ketchup
- Juice drained from 1-pound 4-ounce can pineapple chunks)

Meat and Vegetables
- 3 pounds cooked pork roast
- 1 bunch green onions, chopped
- 1 green pepper, cubed
- 1 cup sliced celery
- 1 1-pound 4-ounce can pineapple chunks, drained (reserve liquid)
- 1 8-ounce can water chestnuts, sliced and well drained

To serve:
- Hot cooked white rice

Shake all sauce ingredients in jar until blended. Dice roast pork. Combine pork and vegetables in large pan. Add sauce to pan. Heat until vegetables are cooked but still crisp. Serve over hot rice.

Makes 6 servings.

VEAL SCALLOPINE WITH CHEESE

Senator **Lowell Weicker, Jr.**—*Connecticut*

2 pounds veal scallops (thin slices)
8 tablespoons (½ cup) butter, divided
3 tablespoons Marsala wine
1 tablespoon all-purpose white flour
½ cup milk
½ cup water
1 chicken bouillon cube
¼ teaspoon ground nutmeg
   Freshly ground black pepper to taste
½ pound Gruyère cheese, grated

Lightly pound veal. Heat 6 tablespoons butter and sauté veal until brown on both sides. Remove veal to flat casserole. Add Marsala to veal juices; cook for a few seconds and set aside.

To prepare sauce, melt remaining 2 tablespoons butter in a saucepan. Add flour and whisk until well blended. Boil water and milk; add bouillon cube and stir until dissolved. Add water-milk mixture to butter and flour and stir until thickened. Season with nutmeg and pepper. Stir in Marsala and veal juices.

Pour sauce over meat. Top with grated cheese. Bake in preheated 425-degree oven until cheese melts and browns.

Makes 8 servings.

CITRUS LAMB

Senator **Thomas F. Eagleton**—*Missouri*
Recipe from: Mrs. Eagleton

1 **5- to 6-pound leg of lamb**
Salt to taste
Black pepper to taste
Paprika to taste
Juice of 1 lemon
2 **onions, sliced**
2 **stalks celery, sliced**
1 **cup water**
3 **tablespoons butter**
2 **tablespoons Worcestershire sauce**
½ **cup chili sauce**
½ **cup orange marmalade**

Sprinkle lamb with salt, pepper, paprika, and lemon juice. Place onions and celery in bottom of roaster. Add water and butter, and set lamb on top of vegetables. Roast in preheated 325-degree oven for 30 minutes. Combine Worcestershire sauce and chili sauce and pour them over lamb. Baste frequently, adding water if needed. Allow 30 minutes per pound for complete roasting time. Spread marmalade over lamb for glaze and return to oven for last 30 minutes.

Makes 5 servings.

Chapter 7

Poultry & Seafood

Chicken

Cornish Hens

Duck

Shellfish

Fish

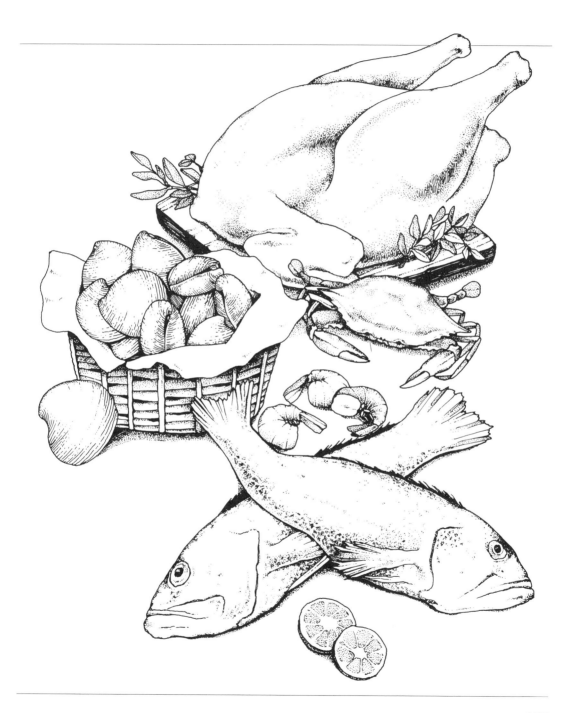

COUNTRY CAPTAIN CHICKEN

Representative **Lindsay Thomas**—*Georgia*
Recipe from: Melinda Thomas

Georgians claim this dish, insisting that a mysterious captain drifted into Savannah due to the spice trade and entrusted his recipe to southern friends. It was a favorite dish of General George Patton while stationed in Columbus, Georgia.

2 large hens (or 4- to 5-pound roasting chickens)
2 medium-sized green peppers
2 small onions
2 cloves garlic
2 tablespoons butter or margarine
1 tablespoon curry powder
2 teaspoons dried thyme leaves
  Salt to taste
  Black pepper to taste
4 cups canned tomatoes
3 4-ounce cans mushrooms, drained
½ pound (8 ounces) blanched almonds, toasted
½ pound (8 ounces) currants or raisins
To serve:
  Hot cooked white rice
  Chutney, chopped peanuts, chopped onions, raisins, crumbled bacon, etc., each served separately

Cut up chicken and steam until tender. While chicken is steaming, cut up peppers, onions, and garlic, and sauté in butter in skillet until slightly brown but not tender. Add to this, curry powder, thyme, salt, pepper, tomatoes, and mushrooms. When well blended, add cooked chicken and half of blanched and toasted almonds, and half of raisins; cook together for 1 hour. (Do not thicken gravy.)

When ready to serve, pour mixture over cooked rice, or place rice around it and sprinkle remaining almonds and raisins over top. Serve with chutney and other assorted condiments and garnishes. (The more the better.)

Makes 8 to 10 servings.

CHICKEN BOG

Representative **Robin Tallon**—*South Carolina*
Recipe from: Mrs. Tallon

Chicken Bog is very popular in the Pee Dee part of South Carolina. During election time, crowds gather in certain areas for a stump meeting where all the candidates speak. It is a low country tradition to serve Chicken Bog at these gatherings.

This is a real family favorite! Serve with cole slaw.

2 **3- to 4-pound fryer chickens**
  Salt to taste
  Black pepper to taste
4 **cups uncooked rice, 2 white and 2 yellow rice with saffron**
4 **tablespoons (½ stick) butter or margarine**
4 **hard-boiled eggs, sliced**
8 **link sausages, fried and halved**
½ **stick butter or margarine**
  Celery seeds to taste

Cover chickens with water in large pot. Add salt and pepper. Boil until tender. Cool chicken and remove from bones; reserve stock. For every cup of raw rice add 2 cups reserved chicken stock. Add chicken and butter and bring to boil. Add sliced eggs and sausage. Lower heat to medium. After rice has swelled, toss a few times, adding more black pepper and celery seeds. Let simmer on low or medium-low until all liquid is absorbed. Serve hot.

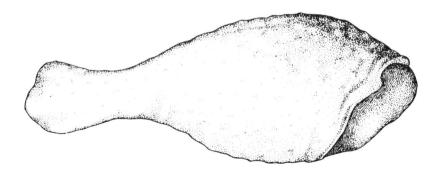

CHICKEN IN THE POT

Representative **Bob Wise**—*West Virginia*
Recipe from: Sandy Wise

>   1 **3-pound chicken**
>   3 **carrots, scraped, split lengthwise and**
>   **cut into 1½-inch lengths**
>   3 **stalks celery, split lengthwise and cut**
>   **into 1½-inch lengths**
> 2 or 3 **turnips, trimmed and cut into long**
>   **pieces about the same size as**
>   **carrots**
>   1 **cup well-washed leeks, quartered**
>   **and cut into 1½-inch lengths**
>   1 **zucchini, trimmed, quartered and cut**
>   **into 1½-inch lengths**
>   6 **cups chicken stock or canned chicken**
>   **broth**
>   ¼ **cup uncooked white rice**
>   **Salt to taste**
>   **Freshly ground black pepper to taste**

Truss chicken and place in kettle. (It should fit snugly or there will be too much water.) Cover with water and add all vegetables, except zucchini. Bring to a full boil.

Drain off all water from kettle and add chicken broth. Simmer 20 minutes. Add zucchini. Simmer 5 minutes longer. Add rice, salt and pepper. Cook 10 minutes or until tender. Untruss chicken. Cut it into pieces and serve along with vegetables.

Makes 4 servings.

JIM'S FAVORITE OVEN-BARBECUED CHICKEN

Senator **James T. Broyhill**—*North Carolina*

7 chicken breast halves
Hot water
3 medium-sized onions
1½ cups tomato juice
¼ teaspoon cayenne pepper
2 teaspoons salt
¼ teaspoon black pepper
¼ teaspoon dry mustard
4½ teaspoons Worcestershire sauce
1 bay leaf
1 teaspoon granulated sugar
¾ cup apple cider vinegar
3 peeled cloves garlic, chopped
½ stick butter

Place chicken breasts in baking pan, being sure to cover bottom of pan with hot water so chicken won't stick. Peel and slice onions thinly over chicken. Bake in preheated 350-degree oven, uncovered, for 30 minutes. Turn chicken over and bake another 30 minutes.

Meanwhile, prepare barbecue sauce by combining all remaining ingredients in saucepan. Simmer 10 minutes. Add barbecue sauce to chicken (turned right side up again), and bake 1 hour longer, or until fork tender. Baste frequently during baking.

Makes 7 servings.

CHINESE CHICKEN WITH WALNUTS

Senator **Albert Gore, Jr.**—*Tennessee*
Recipe from: Tipper Gore

1½ pounds whole chicken breasts, skinned, boned and split
3 tablespoons soy sauce
2 teaspoons cornstarch
2 tablespoons dry sherry
1 teaspoon granulated sugar
1 teaspoon grated fresh gingerroot
½ crushed hot red pepper (or to taste)
½ teaspoon salt
2 tablespoons vegetable oil (approximately)
2 medium-sized green peppers, cut into ¾-inch pieces
4 green onions, bias-sliced into 1-inch lengths
½ cup walnut halves

Cut chicken into 1-inch pieces. Set aside. Blend soy sauce into cornstarch; stir in sherry, sugar, gingerroot, red pepper, and salt.

Preheat wok or large skillet over high heat; add oil. Stir-fry green peppers and onions in hot oil for 2 minutes. Remove. Add walnuts to wok; stir-fry 1 to 2 minutes or until golden. Remove. Add more oil if needed. Add half of chicken pieces; stir-fry for 2 minutes. Remove. Stir-fry remaining chicken pieces for 2 minutes. Return chicken to wok. Stir soy mixture and add to chicken. Cook and stir until bubbly. Stir in vegetables and walnuts; cover and cook for 1 minute.

Makes 6 servings.

ORIENTAL-STYLE CHICKEN WITH PEANUTS

Representative **Dan Rostenkowski**—*Illinois*

1	**pound cubed boneless, skinless chicken breasts (uncooked)**
2⅓	**tablespoons soy sauce, divided**
½	**teaspoon granulated sugar**
1	**teaspoon sesame oil**
1	**teaspoon rice wine or sherry (optional)**
1	**egg white**
1	**tablespoon cornstarch**
3	**tablespoons vegetable oil**
1 to 5	**red or green hot peppers, seeded and finely chopped**
	About 5 cloves garlic, finely chopped
	½-inch piece fresh gingerroot, finely chopped
½	**teaspoon salt**
1	**medium-sized green pepper, cut into 1-inch pieces**
½	**cup roasted peanuts**
2	**scallions, cut into ½-inch pieces (optional)**

To serve:

Hot cooked white rice

Mix chicken with 1⅓ tablespoons soy sauce, sugar, sesame oil, wine, egg white and cornstarch and set aside 1 hour.

Using a large wok or skillet, heat oil. Stir-fry hot peppers, garlic, ginger, and salt; remove after 10 seconds and set aside. Put chicken and marinade in wok and stir-fry until chicken is almost all white. Add green pepper and remaining 1 tablespoon soy sauce and finish cooking chicken; add a little water if mixture becomes too dry. Add peanuts and scallions and cook another 30 seconds; do not overcook or peanuts will become mushy. Serve over rice.

Makes 4 servings.

SWEET AND SOUR CHICKEN

Senator **Paul Simon**—*Illinois*
Recipe from: Jeanne Simon

This recipe is one of Paul's and my favorites. He likes the taste, and I like the fact that it doesn't require long hours in the kitchen.

Sweet and Sour Chicken makes a great buffet supper dish; I serve it with rice and a green salad.

1 **8-ounce bottle Wishbone Russian dressing**
1 **envelope dry onion soup mix**
1 **10-ounce jar apricot preserves**
4 **whole chicken breasts, split in halves**

Combine Russian dressing, soup mix and preserves. Place chicken breasts in well-greased, large, shallow baking dish. Pour sauce over chicken. Bake in preheated 350-degree oven for 1½ hours. Baste twice.

Makes 4 to 6 servings.

TERIYAKI BARBECUED CHICKEN

Representative **Jim Bates**—*California*
Recipe from: Mrs. Bates

   16 **pieces chicken (legs, thighs, wings)**
    1 **medium-sized onion, sliced**
    1 **medium-sized green pepper, sliced**
    1 **10-ounce bottle teriyaki sauce**
    1 **cup white wine**

Arrange chicken, onion, and pepper in shallow noncorrosive pan. Pour teriyaki sauce and white wine over chicken and mix well; be sure all pieces are covered with sauce. Cover and marinate in refrigerator for 24 hours.

Place chicken on charcoal grill and barbecue slowly until chicken is done. If chicken becomes too brown before cooked through, it may be placed in shallow ovenproof dish and baked in 350-degree oven until thoroughly done.

Cook remaining marinade in saucepan over low heat approximately 15 minutes. This may be used on chicken if desired, or as a sauce over rice, if served with meal.

SOY-GINGER CHICKEN

Representative **Beverly Byron**—*Maryland*

> 1 tablespoon sesame seeds
> 1 cup soy sauce
> 1 cup light brown sugar, packed
> 1 small piece gingerroot, crushed or minced
> 2 cloves garlic, crushed or minced
> 1 teaspoon Accent
> 2 tablespoons wine
> 18 chicken thighs

Lightly brown sesame seeds in a skillet. Crush seeds. Combine with all remaining ingredients, except chicken. Pour mixture over chicken pieces and marinate, covered, in refrigerator for 1 hour.

Place chicken pieces skin side up in baking dish. Baste and bake in preheated 350-degree oven for 20 minutes. Turn over chicken and bake 20 minutes longer.

CHICKEN IN WINE

Representative **Morris K. Udall**—*Arizona*

2½ to 3 **pounds chicken pieces**
      Enough white wine to cover chicken
  2 **tablespoons fresh snipped parsley**
      leaves
  2 **tablespoons chopped scallions**
  ½ **cup melted butter**
      Salt to taste
      Black pepper to taste
      Paprika to taste
To serve:
      Hot cooked white rice

Marinate chicken covered in white wine for 3 to 4 hours in refrigerator. Remove chicken and add remaining ingredients to wine.

Place chicken in ovenproof dish and pour over wine mixture. Season with salt, pepper and paprika. Roast in preheated 425-degree oven, skin side down for 30 minutes. Baste if desired. Turn chicken and cook 30 minutes longer. Serve with rice.

GOOD NEIGHBOR CHICKEN

Senator **Mark O. Hatfield**—*Oregon*
Recipe from: Antoinette Kuzmanich Hatfield, in
More ReMARKable Recipes

  ½ **pound dried chipped ham**
  8 **slices bacon**
  4 **whole chicken breasts, boned and**
    halved
  1 **10½-ounce can cream of mushroom**
    soup
½ to 1 **teaspoon curry powder, to taste**
  1 **pint commercial sour cream *or***
    ½ **soup can cooking sherry**

Tear chipped ham in small bits and scatter in bottom
of casserole. Wrap a slice of bacon around each piece
of chicken. Secure with toothpick. Place on chipped
ham. Mix together soup, curry powder and sour
cream. Pour mixture over chicken. Bake, uncovered,
in 300-degree oven for 3 hours.

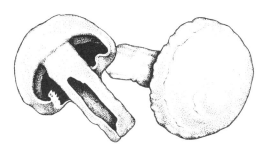

CHICKEN SUPREME

Representative **Delbert L. Latta**—*Ohio*

Chicken Supreme is one of my favorite dishes and has been enjoyed time and time again in the Latta household.
—Delbert L. Latta

1 **glass container chipped beef**
6 **chicken breast halves, boned**
6 **strips bacon**
1 **10½-ounce can cream of mushroom soup**
1 **cup commercial sour cream**
1 **4-ounce can mushrooms, drained**

To serve:
Hot cooked white rice

Line casserole with beef. Roll chicken breasts in slices of bacon and place on top of beef. Blend together sour cream and soup. Pour over chicken. Sprinkle mushrooms over top. Cover with foil and bake in preheated 275-degree oven for 3 hours. Serve over rice.

Makes 6 servings.

CHICKEN FLORENTINE

Representative **Dick Cheney**—*Wyoming*

    4 whole, unsplit, boneless chicken
         breasts with or without skin (about
         2½ pounds)
       Salt to taste
       Black pepper to taste
    2 tablespoons plus 2 teaspoons butter,
         divided
    1 tablespoon finely chopped shallots
    ½ cup dry white wine
    ½ cup chicken broth
    2 sprigs fresh parsley
    2 10-ounce packages fresh spinach
    2 tablespoons all-purpose white flour
    1 cup heavy cream
    1 egg yolk, lightly beaten
1 or 2 tablespoons grated Gruyère or
         Parmesan cheese

Place chicken breasts on a flat surface, opened out, skin side down. Sprinkle with salt and pepper. Fold chicken breasts, seasoned surfaces together, reshaping them skin side out. Smooth skin over. Butter bottom of a skillet with 2 teaspoons butter and sprinkle with shallots. Add reshaped breasts, seam side down. Add wine, chicken broth, salt and pepper. Add parsley and bring to a boil. Cover and simmer 15 to 20 minutes, until breasts are just cooked through. Remove from heat.

As chicken cooks, prepare spinach according to package. Drain and reserve all cooking liquid from chicken breasts; there should be about 1½ cups. Cover chicken; set aside.

Heat remaining 2 tablespoons butter in saucepan. Add flour, stirring with a wire whisk until blended. Add reserved cooking liquid to butter-flour mixture, stirring with whisk. When thickened and smooth, simmer about 5 minutes. Add cream and cook about 2 minutes. Remove from heat and add egg yolk, stirring briskly. Preheat broiler. Spoon spinach into center of heatproof serving dish. Arrange chicken breasts seam side down over spinach. Spoon sauce over chicken and spinach. Sprinkle cheese on top and run under broiler until bubbling on top.

Makes 4 servings.

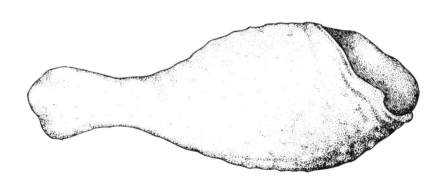

CHICKEN CROQUETTES (OR FRITTERS OR APPETIZERS)

Representative **Jaime B. Fuster**—*Puerto Rico*

    2 pounds chicken breasts
    4 cups water
    2 tablespoons salt
    3 coriander leaves
    1 garlic clove
    ½ medium-sized onion
      Chili peppers to taste
    6 tablespoons butter or margarine
    ½ cup all-purpose white flour
      Salt to taste
    ¼ teaspoon white pepper
    1½ cups whole milk
    1⅓ cups cracker crumbs
    3 eggs, beaten
      Oil or margarine for frying

Bring chicken to boil in water with 2 tablespoons salt, coriander, garlic, onion, and chili pepper. Simmer for 30 minutes. Remove chicken from liquid. Cool and dice chicken. (There should be about 2½ cups.)

Melt butter in saucepan over low heat. Add ½ cup flour, salt to taste and pepper, stirring with wooden spoon to form soft paste. Over medium heat, stir in milk; cook, stirring, until boiling. (Mixture will thicken.) Add chicken and continue cooking until mixture leaves sides of pan. Turn mixture out onto platter to cool. Using a spoon, shape portions of mixture into croquettes; roll between palms to smooth. (Smaller portions may be shaped to form fritters or appetizers.) Coat croquettes with crumbs. Dip in eggs; then coat with crumbs again. Let stand on platter for 15 minutes, or cover and refrigerate overnight. Fry over medium heat until cooked through and golden brown. Drain on paper towels.

CROCKPOT CORNISH HENS

Senator **Don Nickles**—*Oklahoma*

> 1 8-ounce package cornbread stuffing
> 3 Cornish hens, rinsed and patted dry
> ¼ cup melted butter
> 2 tablespoons light brown sugar, packed
> 2 tablespoons lime juice
> 2 tablespoons dry white wine
> 2 tablespoons soy sauce

Prepare cornbread stuffing as directed on package. Stuff hens. Combine all remaining ingredients until well mixed. Brush sauce on hens. Arrange hens in crockpot, neck down. Cover and cook hens on low setting for 5 to 7 hours, occasionally basting with sauce.

OVEN-BRAISED WILD DUCK

Representative **Beryl Anthony, Jr.**—*Arkansas*

Being an avid hunter and sportsman, I enjoy trying new game dishes. The following is one of my favorites.

3 cups sherry
¼ cup vegetable oil
1 cup water
2 tablespoons (¼ stick) butter
½ teaspoon dried red (hot) pepper
1 teaspoon white pepper
1 tablespoon chopped fresh parsley
2 bottles onion juice
3 wild ducks
1 onion, quartered
3 bay leaves
Salt to taste

Combine all ingredients except ducks, onion, bay leaves and salt in deep Dutch oven. Bring to a boil. Salt ducks inside and out. Put onion quarter and bay leaf inside each duck cavity. Place ducks in liquid and cover. Cook 3 hours in preheated 350-degree oven. (If preferred, simmer on top of stove.) Cool until ducks can be handled. Cut in half.

Makes 6 servings.

DEVILED CRABMEAT CASSEROLE

Representative **Marjorie S. Holt**—*Maryland*

Maryland and crabs have long been synonymous. The Chesapeake Bay is the world's largest producer of Blue Channel crabs, and they are recognized throughout the nation as an epicurean treat.

3 **eggs**
5 **tablespoons butter, divided**
2 **tablespoons all-purpose white flour**
2½ **cups milk**
2 **tablespoons chopped parsley**
1 **teaspoon minced onion**
2 **cups diced fresh crabmeat, all shell removed**
1¼ **teaspoon salt**
¼ **teaspoon paprika**
2 **tablespoons sherry or Worcestershire sauce (optional)**
⅓ **cup bread crumbs**

Boil eggs until hard-cooked. Shell them. Separate yolks from whites. While still hot, crush yolks with a fork, or rice them. Blend them with 1½ tablespoons butter. Blend 2 tablespoons flour and another 1½ tablespoons butter. Combine yolk and flour mixture. Then, stir in milk slowly. Cook mixture, stirring, over low heat until it thickens and boils. Add chopped egg whites, parsley, onion, crabmeat, salt, paprika and sherry, mixing gently but thoroughly. Pour mixture into greased casserole. Cover top with bread crumbs. Dot with remaining 2 tablespoons butter. Bake in preheated 500-degree oven for about 10 minutes.

Makes 10 servings.

VIRGINIA CRAB IMPERIAL

Senator **Paul Trible**—*Virginia*
Recipe from: Rosemary Trible

  2 **eggs, beaten**
  ¼ **teaspoon dry mustard**
      Dash white pepper
  2 **pounds backfin crabmeat, all shell removed**
  4 **tablespoons chopped pimiento**
2¼ **cups mayonnaise**
  ¼ **cup grated Parmesan cheese**

Preheat oven to 350 degrees. Beat eggs with mustard and pepper. Add crabmeat, pimiento, 2 cups mayonnaise. Spoon mixture into greased 2-quart casserole. Spread ¼ cup mayonnaise over top. Sprinkle with cheese. Bake for 20 minutes in preheated 350-degree oven till brown and bubbly.

Makes 8 servings.

BAKED CRAB IN SHELLS

Senator **Lloyd Bentsen**—*Texas*

It is a pleasure to share my favorite recipe. I hope you enjoy it.

1 medium-sized green pepper, diced
2 cups diced celery
2 cups diced onion
3 to 4 tablespoons butter
1 cup cracker crumbs
2 cups light cream
Salt to taste
Black pepper to taste
Tabasco sauce to taste
1 pound lump crabmeat, all shell removed
Paprika for garnish
Lemon for garnish
Parsley for garnish

Sauté pepper, celery and onion in butter. In a bowl, mix cracker crumbs, cream, salt, pepper and Tabasco sauce. Add sautéed vegetables and crabmeat. Fill 6 to 8 decorative seafood shells; top with paprika. Bake in preheated 350-degree oven for 40 minutes. Garnish with lemon and parsley.

Makes 6 to 8 servings.

MOBILE-STYLE BAKED CRABS

Senator **Jeremiah Denton**—*Alabama*

> 1 medium-sized green pepper, diced
> 4 or 5 parsley sprigs, chopped
> ½ small onion, chopped
> 6 stalks celery, finely chopped
> 1 tablespoon Worcestershire sauce
> Salt to taste
> Black pepper to taste
> Cayenne pepper to taste
> 1 cup heavy white sauce
> 1 cup well seasoned mayonnaise
> 8 thin slices dry toast, crushed to crumbs
> 1 pound lump crabmeat, all shell removed
> 4 hard-boiled eggs, chopped

Combine all ingredients except toast crumbs, crabmeat and eggs and mix well. Add toast crumbs, saving a few for top of crab. Add crabmeat and eggs last; don't stir, fold ingredients together so crabmeat will remain in lumps. Fill 6 decorative seafood shells and top with buttered crumbs. Bake in preheated 350-degree oven for about 20 minutes.

Makes 6 servings.

SHRIMP CREOLE

Senator **Russell B. Long**—*Louisiana*

    2 tablespoons vegetable oil
    1 large onion, minced
    1 clove garlic, minced
    2 tablespoons minced green pepper
    1 tablespoon all-purpose white flour
    1 8-ounce can tomato sauce
1½ to 2 tomato sauce cans water
    Pinch dried thyme leaves
    2 tablespoons minced fresh parsley
    2 pounds fresh shrimp, cleaned and peeled
    1 teaspoon salt
    ½ teaspoon black pepper
    Dash cayenne pepper

To serve:
    Hot cooked white rice

Heat oil over medium heat; add onion and cook until soft, about 6 to 8 minutes. Stir in garlic and green pepper; sauté 2 minutes. Stir in flour until well blended. Add tomato sauce and simmer 5 minutes. Stir in water, thyme, parsley, shrimp, salt, pepper, and cayenne pepper. Cover and simmer 30 minutes. Serve over rice.

Makes 4 servings.

P. A.'S BAKED SHRIMP

Representative **Trent Lott**—*Mississippi*

Serve this dish with salad, French garlic bread and plenty of napkins.

5 pounds medium to large shrimp, heads off but in shells
½ to 1 small bottle Worcestershire sauce
1 tablespoon salt
1 21-ounce bottle ketchup
1 teaspoon horseradish
Juice of 1 lemon

Wash shrimp and drain. Place in oblong noncorrosive baking dish. Mix all ingredients and pour over shrimp, stirring every 15 to 20 minutes; do not cover. Bake in preheated 350-degree oven for 1 hour or until shrimp begin to pull away from shells. Guests peel their own shrimp.*

Note: Peel shrimp by pulling tail off, then grabbing legs and pulling off with shell in one round motion.

Makes 8 servings.

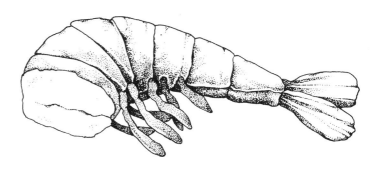

RED SPANISH
SCAMPI PROVENÇALE

Representative **Henry J. Hyde**—*Illinois*

8 jumbo red Spanish shrimp
All-purpose white flour
Salt to taste
White pepper to taste
3 or 4 tablespoons clarified butter
3 ripe tomatoes, peeled and chopped
6 tablespoons butter
1 tablespoon fresh parsley, chopped
½ clove garlic, chopped

Clean, devein and butterfly shrimp. Dust with flour; season with salt and pepper. In a pan large enough to hold shrimp without crowding, heat clarified butter and gently cook shrimp over moderate heat until nicely golden. Add chopped tomatoes and cook for approximately 3 minutes. Remove from heat and add butter, parsley and garlic. Keep pan and its ingredients moving over high heat until all the butter has been incorporated into tomatoes. Serve dish along with boiled potatoes.

Makes 2 servings.

SHRIMP FLORENTINE

Representative **J. Roy Rowland**—*Georgia*
Recipe from: Mrs. Rowland

> 3 **10-ounce packages frozen chopped spinach, thawed**
> **Garlic powder to taste (optional)**
> **Onion powder to taste (optional)**
> 2 **pounds shrimp, cooked**
> **Sauce**
> 1 **cup commercial sour cream (or plain yogurt)**
> ½ **cup mayonnaise**
> ½ **cup finely chopped onion**
> **Paprika for garnish**
> **Grated Parmesan cheese for garnish (optional)**

Drain and heat spinach. Add onion powder or garlic powder, if desired. Put spinach in greased casserole. Top with shrimp. Bake in preheated 350-degree oven for about 15 minutes.

Stir together sour cream, mayonnaise and onion. Spread over shrimp. Sprinkle top with paprika and Parmesan cheese, if desired, and bake at 500 degrees about 15 minutes longer or until hot and bubbly.

Makes 6 servings.

CONCH IN BUTTER SAUCE

Representative **Ron De Lugo**—*Virgin Islands*

Conch is a longtime favorite dish of U.S. Virgin Islanders. Conch comes from the shellfish family, and it is found in tropical waters.
—Ron De Lugo

2 to 3 **pounds conch meat, cubed**
3 **cups water**
2 **tablespoons lemon juice**
1 to 2 **onions, sliced**
2 **sticks butter or margarine**
½ **cup apple cider vinegar**
Dash cayenne pepper
Salt to taste
Black pepper to taste

Boil conch in water several hours or until tender. Drain conch, reserving ½ cup cooking liquid. Combine conch, reserved cooking liquid and all remaining ingredients and simmer 1 hour over low heat.

SEAFOOD MARINARA

Representative **Ray McGrath**—*New York*

The following is one of my favorites.

1 large onion, chopped
1 garlic clove, minced
2 tablespoons olive or vegetable oil
3 16-ounce cans tomatoes, crushed
1 small can tomato puree
¼ cup white wine
  Tabasco sauce to taste
3 large pieces fresh flounder, filleted
1 pound peeled fresh shrimp
1 pound fresh scallops

To serve:
  Hot cooked linguine or rice

Sauté onion and garlic in oil over medium heat for about 10 minutes. Add tomatoes, puree, wine and Tabasco. Bring sauce to boil; cover and simmer about 1 hour. Meanwhile, ready seafood. Cut fish into good-sized chunks; skin can be left on since it will fall off when cooked. Rinse and drain shrimp and scallops.

When sauce is ready, place fish in sauce, but do not stir. Cover and let cook about 25 minutes. Add scallops and shrimp and cook 10 to 15 minutes longer.

Serve over linguine or rice.

Makes 6 servings.

GREAT BARBECUED KENAI SALMON

Senator **Frank Murkowski**—*Alaska*

There is nothing better than fresh Alaskan salmon!

½ cup apple cider
6 tablespoons soy sauce
2 tablespoons butter
1 large garlic clove, crushed
2 salmon fillets, each 2⅓ to 3 pounds; or a 4- to 5-pound salmon steak, cut 1-inch thick

Prepare a marinade by combining cider and soy sauce. Bring to a boil and reduce heat. Simmer 3 minutes. Add butter and garlic and continue cooking. Simmer, stirring occasionally, until liquid reduces and thickens enough to coat back of a spoon, about 20 minutes. Cool.

Brush marinade over salmon fillets and place skin side down on rack. Let stand 30 minutes at room temperature. Cook on hot coals; make an aluminum foil tent over fish. Bake for 15 to 20 minutes, until fish is tender and just flakes.

WASHINGTON BARBECUED SALMON

Representative **Mike Lowry**—*Washington*

1 **5- to 8-pound whole dressed fresh or frozen salmon, thawed if necessary**
Salt to taste
Black pepper to taste
2 **tablespoons butter or margarine, softened**
½ **medium-sized onion, sliced**
½ **medium-sized lemon, sliced**
2 or 3 **sprigs fresh parsley**
Vegetable or olive oil
Lemon wedges for garnish

Wash salmon and pat dry. Sprinkle inside of salmon with salt and pepper; dot with butter. Arrange onion, lemon slices and parsley leaves in overlapping fashion in cavity. Brush salmon with oil. Wrap in heavy-duty aluminum foil; seal edges with double fold.

Place on grill over medium-hot coals. Carefully turn salmon every 10 minutes. Test for doneness after 45 minutes by inserting meat thermometer in thickest part. Cook to internal temperature of 160 degrees, or until salmon flakes easily when tested with a fork at thickest part. To serve, transfer salmon to serving platter and fold back foil. Cut between bone and meat with a wide spatula; lift off each serving. Serve with lemon wedges.

Makes 8 to 12 servings.

SWORDFISH EN BROCHETTE

Senator **John H. Chafee**—*Rhode Island*

4 pounds skinless, boneless swordfish
1 medium-sized onion, chopped
  Pinch of dried thyme leaves
  Pinch of dried tarragon leaves
1 bay leaf
  Juice of 1 lemon
  Corn oil
4 medium-sized green peppers
1 pound fresh button mushrooms
  Butter
  Salt to taste
  Ground black pepper to taste
To serve:
  Hot cooked white rice

Cut swordfish into cubes approximately 2 ounces each (allowing 4 cubes per person). Place cubes in a bowl and add onion, thyme, tarragon, bay leaf and lemon juice. Cover with corn oil and let marinate in refrigerator overnight. Cut green pepper into quarters and remove seeds. Boil green pepper quarters for 5 minutes (with a touch of baking soda to keep color); drain. Sauté mushroom caps in butter with a drop of lemon juice for 5 minutes. Remove swordfish cubes from oil and place on skewers, alternating with mushrooms and green peppers. Sprinkle with salt and pepper, and broil for 15 minutes, turning frequently. Serve on rice.

Makes 6 to 8 servings.

SALMON TARTARE

Senator **Mark O. Hatfield**—*Oregon*

Court bouillon and fish

- 8 cups water
- 1 medium-sized onion, chopped
- 1 medium-sized carrot, chopped
- 3 stalks celery, chopped
- 1 bay leaf
- 2 sprigs parsley
- 6 peppercorns
- 1 tablespoon salt
- 2 whole cloves
- 2 tablespoons white vinegar
- 1 6-pound dressed salmon with head and tail intact

Sauce tartare

- ½ large Bermuda onion
- 2 hard-cooked egg yolks
- 1 green pepper
- 2 dill pickles (with garlic)
- 2 cups mayonnaise
- ¼ cup chili sauce
- ¼ bottle prepared horseradish
- 1 tablespoon capers
- ½ clove garlic, minced
- Salt to taste
- Black pepper to taste
- Dash cayenne pepper
- ½ cup commercial sour cream

Garnish

- Hard-cooked egg whites
- Dungeness crab

Prepare court bouillon for poaching fish by combining all ingredients except vinegar and fish in a large noncorrosive kettle. Bring ingredients to a boil. Add vinegar. Simmer liquid, covered, for 30 minutes; strain.

Wrap fish in cheesecloth. Lay on rack in fish kettle and add court bouillon to cover. Bring to boil and simmer gently, 10 to 12 minutes per pound. Remove carefully from liquid and unwrap cheesecloth, laying fish on platter covered with paper towels to absorb liquid. Chill fish.

Put first 4 sauce ingredients through a food chopper (or finely chop in food processor). Then add all remaining sauce ingredients, stirring until well mixed. Refrigerate. A few hours before serving, arrange fish on serving platter. Mask carefully with sauce. Sprinkle on egg whites. Garnish with Dungeness crab. Refrigerate until serving time.

MAINE HADDOCK FILLETS

Representative **John R. McKernan, Jr.**—*Maine*

> 2 **pounds haddock fillets**
> ½ **teaspoon salt**
> ¼ **teaspoon black pepper**
> ¼ **teaspoon paprika**
> ¼ **cup lemon juice**
> **Sauce**
> 2 **tablespoons butter**
> 2 **tablespoons all-purpose white flour**
> 1 **tablespoon dry mustard**
> 1 **cup milk**
> **Salt to taste**
> **Black pepper to taste**
> **Topping**
> ½ **cup buttered crumbs**
> 1 **tablespoon chopped fresh parsley**

Lay fish in shallow baking dish. Season with salt, pepper, paprika, and lemon juice.

To prepare sauce, melt butter. Stir in flour until well blended. Stir in mustard. Gradually add milk, stirring until smooth. Add salt and pepper and cook slowly in saucepan over low heat, stirring constantly until thickened. Pour sauce over seasoned fish. Top with buttered crumbs. Bake in preheated 350-degree oven for 35 minutes. Sprinkle with chopped parsley.

Makes 6 servings.

FISH CHOWDER
ON-THE-GRILL

Representative **Bill Chappell**—*Florida*

For each serving:

- 1 **cup fish chunks (preferably rock, pompano, grouper, red snapper, etc.)**
- ¼ **cup finely chopped onion**
- ½ **cup cubed vegetables (potatoes, carrots, celery)**
- ½ **teaspoon salt**
- ⅛ **teaspoon black pepper**
- ½ **teaspoon Worcestershire sauce**
- ⅛ **teaspoon Tabasco sauce (or to taste)**
- ½ **tablespoon ketchup**
  Dash of cavenders (Greek spice)

Prepare charcoal for grilling. When coals are hot, place each serving on a square of heavy-duty aluminum foil. Wrap, twisting ends to seal securely. Cook on grill, for approximately 45 minutes, until vegetables are tender. Serve piping hot.

ESKABECHI

Representative **Ben Blaz**—*Guam*

Surrounded by the beautiful blue Pacific Ocean, the island of Guam has an abundance of seafood. Fresh vegetables are also always available year round and are used for many other special island dishes prepared by the natives of Guam. Eskabechi is prepared during special occasions such as fandangos (weddings), christenings, and village fiestas. Eskabechi is especially served during the Lenten season. Eskabechi may be made from different kinds of fish, such as parrot fish, tuna, yellow fin, etc.

1 medium-sized fish (1½ to 2½ pounds), dressed
Salt to taste
Oil or butter
1 garlic clove, minced
1 large onion, cut into lengthwise slices
¼ cup chopped fresh gingerroot
2 cups green papaya, chopped
1 medium-sized green pepper, sliced
2 eggplants, sliced
½ head cabbage, quartered
6 green beans, cut in 1-inch lengths
2 fresh tomatoes, sliced
3 green onions, including tops, chopped
⅓ cup apple cider vinegar
1 cup water
2 tablespoons soy sauce
1 tablespoon cornstarch
2 tablespoons cold water

To serve:

Hot cooked white rice

Sprinkle clean fish with salt inside and out. Let stand for 10 minutes. Sauté fish in oil or butter until just cooked through. Cut in 3 pieces and set aside to keep warm while sauce is prepared.

Saute garlic and onions until onions are soft in large pot. Add gingerroot, papaya, green pepper, eggplants, cabbage and beans, and cook another 10 minutes over medium heat. Add tomatoes and green onions and cook briefly. Add vinegar, water and soy sauce. Bring to boil. Stir cornstarch into 2 tablespoons cold water. Stir into pot and allow sauce to thicken. Spoon over warm fish. Return fish to warm stove and allow to stand for about 5 minutes to allow flavors to penetrate fish. Serve with hot rice.

Makes 2 or 3 servings.

Chapter 8

Breads

Yeast Breads

Quick Breads

Pancakes & Crepes

SWEDISH RYE BREAD

Representative **Charles Stenholm**—*Texas*

3 cups milk
3 tablespoons butter
1 cup molasses
2 packages active dry yeast
¼ cup lukewarm water
¼ cup plus 2 tablespoons granulated
   sugar
1 tablespoon salt
2 cups rye flour
6 to 8 cups sifted all-purpose white flour

Scald milk, but do not boil. Add butter and molasses to the milk and let it cool. Combine yeast and lukewarm water. Stir sugar and salt into yeast mixture. Add yeast mixture to cool milk. Add rye flour to liquid. Gradually add white flour to mixture. Knead dough on floured board.

Let dough rise, covered, in greased bowl until doubled in size. Punch down and shape into 3 loaves. Let dough rise again, covered, in greased and floured loaf pans, or 1-pound coffee cans.

Bake in preheated 325-degree oven for about 45 minutes or until done. Loaves may be frozen.

Makes 3 loaves.

BROWN BREAD

Representative **Rick Boucher**—*Virginia*

1 cup brown sugar, packed
1 cup dark molasses
3 packages active dry yeast
2 tablespoons salt
2 cups nonfat dry milk powder
7 cups very warm water
5 tablespoons melted butter or
   margarine
3 eggs, lightly beaten
9 cups whole wheat flour
   Approximately 8 cups all-purpose
   white flour

Mix together all ingredients except white flour and let stand for 15 minutes. Work in enough white flour to make elastic dough. Cover and let rise until double in bulk. Punch down dough and let rise again. Shape into 5 loaves and let rise in greased loaf pans until more than double.

Bake in preheated 350-degree oven until done, about 40 minutes.

Makes 5 loaves.

FLOWER POT BREAD

Senator **J. James Exon**—*Nebraska*

This is an Easter tradition.

6 3-inch clay flower pots
1 package active dry yeast
½ cup warm water
⅛ teaspoon ground ginger
3 tablespoons granulated sugar,
   divided
1 13-ounce can evaporated milk
1 teaspoon salt
2 tablespoons vegetable oil
4 to 4½ cups all-purpose white flour

Season pots by baking at 425 degrees for 30 minutes. Grease them well with vegetable oil and repeat a second time. (Once pots are seasoned, this step doesn't have to be repeated.)

Dissolve yeast in water. Stir in ginger and 1 tablespoon sugar. Let stand 15 minutes. Add remaining sugar, milk, salt and oil. Beat in flour 1 cup at a time. Fill pots ½ full. Let dough rise.

Bake in preheated 350-degree oven for 40 to 45 minutes. When done, brush tops with butter and let cool 5 to 10 minutes. Loosen crust with a knife. Bread can be served in pots. Freezes well.

Makes 6 flower pot-sized loaves.

BUTTERHORN ROLLS

Representative **Richard Gephardt**—*Missouri*

This recipe has been used through all the generations in our family and now, my son, Richard, bakes these rolls for many of his dinners when he and his wife, Jane, entertain.
—Loreen Gephardt

1 fresh cake yeast*
1 cup lukewarm water
½ cup granulated sugar
3 eggs, well beaten
¾ cup melted butter
½ teaspoon salt
4 cups all-purpose white flour

Dissolve yeast in water. Add sugar, eggs, butter and salt. Work in flour, mixing well. Cover dough and refrigerate overnight.

Divide dough into thirds. Shape each third into a ball. Roll out ball into circle ¼-inch thick. Cut dough (as if cutting a pie) into wedges. Starting from wider end, roll up wedges to form rolls. Transfer to baking sheet; let rise 2 hours. Bake in preheated 400-degree oven about 15 minutes.

Editor's Note: Since cake yeast is sometimes difficult to find, it may be more convenient to use a package of active dry yeast.

Makes about 2 dozen rolls.

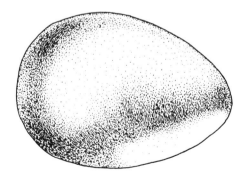

NEW JERSEY BLUEBERRY OR CRANBERRY MUFFINS

Senator **Bill Bradley**—*New Jersey*

Nationally, New Jersey ranks second and third, respectively, in the production of blueberries and cranberries.

2 **cups sifted, unbleached white flour**
½ **cup granulated sugar**
2½ **teaspoons baking powder**
¾ **teaspoon salt**
1 **egg, well beaten**
1 **cup milk**
⅓ **cup vegetable oil**
1 **cup fresh (or thawed and well-drained) blueberries or cranberries**

Sift dry ingredients into bowl; make a well in center. Stir together egg, milk and oil. Add liquid all at once to dry ingredients. Stir quickly, just until dry ingredients are blended. Gently stir in blueberries or cranberries. Fill greased muffin tin cups ⅔ full.

Bake in preheated 400-degree oven for about 25 minutes.

Makes 12 muffins.

MARY'S BRAN MUFFINS

Senator **Mark Andrews**—*North Dakota*

> 1 cup boiling water
> 1 cup chopped dates or raisins
> 2½ teaspoons baking soda
> 1 cup granulated sugar
> 2¾ cups all-purpose white flour
> ½ teaspoon salt
> 2 eggs, lightly beaten
> ½ cup sunflower oil
> 2 cups commercial buttermilk
> 3 to 4 cups unprocessed, hard red spring
>   wheat bran from North Dakota

Pour boiling water over dates and add soda. Add all remaining ingredients; use enough bran to produce a fairly moist, pourable batter. Mix lightly until blended. Pour into muffin tins. Bake in preheated 375-degree oven for 20 minutes.

Note: Makes a large batch. Recipe may be halved, if desired.

Representative **Neal Smith**—*Iowa*

2 cups all-purpose white flour
4 teaspoons baking powder
1 teaspoon salt
7 tablespoons cold margarine
¾ to 1 cup milk

Combine dry ingredients. Cut in margarine thoroughly. Gradually add milk; stir until soft and sticky. Knead dough 10 times. Roll out dough and cut out biscuits.

Bake biscuits 10 minutes in preheated 450-degree oven.

Makes about 12 biscuits.

IRISH SODA BREAD

Representative **Edward F. Feighan**—*Ohio*

A wonderful low sodium, low sugar snack at approximately 88 calories per slice.

3 cups all-purpose white flour
¼ cup granulated sugar
1 teaspoon baking soda
½ teaspoon baking powder
½ teaspoon salt
¼ teaspoon cream of tartar
⅔ cup cold margarine or butter
1⅓ cups commercial buttermilk or sour milk
1 cup raisins or currants
Walnuts to taste (optional)

Stir together dry ingredients. Cut in margarine or butter. Add buttermilk. Add raisins, and walnuts if desired. Mound dough into a loaf. Bake on greased baking sheet in preheated 350-degree oven for 45 to 50 minutes.

Makes 12 to 15 servings.

SPOON BREAD

Representative **G. V. Montgomery**—*Mississippi*

This is a Montgomery family favorite.

½ **cup water**
1 **teaspoon salt**
1 **cup white cornmeal**
2 **tablespoons butter**
1 **cup milk**
2 **eggs, separated**

Bring water and salt to a boil. Gradually stir in cornmeal. When smooth, add butter, milk, and egg yolks. Beat egg whites until stiff. Fold beaten egg whites into mixture. Pour batter into greased baking dish. Bake in preheated 350-degree oven for 30 minutes or until firm. Serve with butter.

JALAPEÑO CORNBREAD

Senator **Paul Laxalt**—*Nevada*

1 cup yellow cornmeal
½ cup all-purpose white flour
½ teaspoon baking soda
1 teaspoon salt
1 cup creamed corn
1 cup commercial buttermilk
1 medium-sized onion, chopped
¼ cup green chili peppers
¼ pound (4 ounces) shredded sharp
    Cheddar cheese
½ cup vegetable oil
2 eggs, slightly beaten

Preheat oven to 425 degrees. Grease 2 large pie plates. Combine all dry ingredients. Stir in corn, buttermilk, onion, peppers and cheese. Add remaining ingredients. Stir until moist. Turn into pie plates. Bake 25 to 30 minutes. Let stand 5 minutes before cutting.

MEXICAN CORNBREAD

Representative **Jack Kemp**—*New York*
Recipe from: Mrs. Kemp

> 1 cup all-purpose white flour
> 1 cup cornmeal
> 4 teaspoons baking powder
> ¼ teaspoon salt
> 1 cup margarine, softened
> 1 cup granulated sugar
> 4 eggs, beaten
> 1 16-ounce can creamed corn
> 1 4-ounce can chopped green chilies
> ½ cup shredded Jack cheese
> ½ cup shredded Cheddar cheese

Preheat oven to 350 degrees. Grease 8 x 12-inch
baking pan.

Stir together flour, cornmeal, baking powder and salt.
Combine all remaining ingredients. Stir into dry
ingredients. Pour into pan. Lower oven heat to 300
degrees and bake for about 55 to 60 minutes.

ORANGE ZUCCHINI BREAD

Representative **Edward Madigan**—*Illinois*
Recipe from: Evelyn Madigan

> 3 eggs
> 1¾ cups granulated sugar
> 1 cup vegetable oil
> 1 tablespoon vanilla extract
> 2 cups raw, unpeeled zucchini, ground or grated
> 1 tablespoon grated orange rind
> 3 cups all-purpose white flour
> 1 teaspoon salt
> 1 teaspoon baking soda
> ¼ teaspoon baking powder
> 2 teaspoons ground cinnamon
> ½ cup chopped nuts

Beat eggs until light and fluffy. Add sugar and beat well. Stir in oil, vanilla, zucchini and orange rind.

Sift together flour, salt, soda, baking powder and cinnamon and stir into other ingredients. Add nuts. Pour into 2 greased and floured 8½ x 4½-inch loaf pans. Bake in preheated 325-degree oven for 50 to 60 minutes or until brown.

Makes 2 loaves.

BANANA BREAD

Representative **Beverly Byron**—*Maryland*

2 cups all-purpose white flour
2 teaspoons baking soda
2 teaspoons ground cinnamon
½ teaspoon salt
1 cup vegetable oil
1½ cups granulated sugar
3 eggs
2 cups mashed, ripe banana*
½ cup walnuts
1 teaspoon vanilla extract

Sift together flour, baking soda, cinnamon and salt. Stir together oil, sugar, eggs, banana, walnuts and vanilla in large bowl. Stir dry ingredients into mixture until well blended. Pour into 2 well-greased and floured loaf pans. Bake in preheated 350-degree oven for 55 to 60 minutes.

Note: Carrot bread can be made by substituting 2 cups grated carrot for banana.

Makes 2 small loaves.

PRINEVILLE PUMPKIN BREAD

Representative **Denny Smith**—*Oregon*

3 cups granulated sugar
3½ cups all-purpose white flour
½ teaspoon salt
2 teaspoons baking soda
1 teaspoon ground cinnamon
1 teaspoon ground nutmeg
4 eggs
½ cup water
1 cup vegetable oil
2 cups pumpkin (canned or fresh)
¼ cup sweet red vermouth or water
1 cup raisins (optional)
½ cup chopped pecans (optional)
Butter and confectioners' sugar
(optional)

Sift dry ingredients into mixing bowl. Make a well and add eggs, water, oil, pumpkin and vermouth. Beat thoroughly with mixer. Add raisins and/or nuts. Grease and flour 3 loaf pans or equivalent. Bake loaves in preheated 350-degree oven for about 1 hour. If desired, spread loaf tops with butter and sprinkle with powdered sugar.

Makes 3 loaves.

LEFSE
(POTATO FLATBREAD)

Representative **Steve Gunderson**—*Wisconsin*

Lefse is a very thin, tasty flatbread that originated in Scandinavia.

2 cups freshly cooked potatoes
2 tablespoons butter
3 tablespoons cream
1 teaspoon salt
1 cup all-purpose white flour

Rice potatoes twice while still hot. Then thoroughly chill potatoes before making into lefse.

Work butter, cream and salt into potatoes until well blended. Then add flour; knead just a little to obtain smooth texture. Divide dough into 6 rounds. Roll each very thin on lightly floured pastry cloth with lefse rolling pin or rolling pin covered with pastry stocking. Cook lefse on moderately hot ungreased griddle. Serve with butter or along with cold meat as a sandwich.

Makes 6 flatbreads.

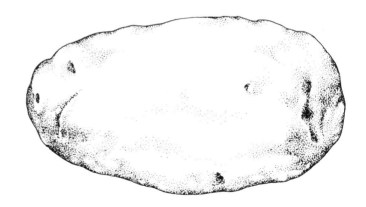

SWEDISH PANCAKES

Representative **Jim Courter**—*New Jersey*
Recipe from: Carmen Courter

Fill the pancakes with your favorite sauces and serve as a dessert or fill with creamed chicken and serve as a lunch.

    3 **eggs**
 1¼ **cups milk**
  ¾ **cup sifted all-purpose white flour**
    1 **tablespoon granulated sugar**
  ½ **teaspoon salt**

Beat eggs till thick and lemon-colored. Stir in milk. Sift together dry ingredients; add to egg mixture, mixing until smooth.

Drop small amount of batter (1 tablespoon for 3-inch cakes) onto moderately hot, buttered griddle (or bake on special Swedish griddle). Spread batter evenly to make thin cakes. Turn when underside is delicately browned. (To keep first pancakes warm, place them on towel-covered baking sheet in very slow oven.)

DAVID EYRE PANCAKE

Representative **Thomas N. Kindness**—*Ohio*

Serve this with bacon or sausage, fruit and a beverage for brunch, or breakfast, or serve as a light supper.

2 **tablespoons butter**
2 **eggs, lightly beaten**
½ **cup milk**
½ **cup all-purpose white flour**
   Pinch nutmeg
   Confectioners' sugar
   Lemon wedges
   Pint of strawberries (optional)
   Granulated sugar (optional)
   Grand Marnier (optional)

Preheat oven to 425 degrees. Place butter in 10-inch ovenproof pie plate to melt in oven. Combine eggs, milk, flour, and nutmeg, mixing lightly. Pour mixture into heated dish and bake for 15 minutes. Pancake should rise about 3 inches above edge. Sprinkle liberally with confectioners' sugar and bake 2 minutes longer.

Serve with fresh lemon, or while baking pancake, macerate slightly mashed strawberries in sugar with Grand Marnier. Drain and serve on pancake; drink juice. (Experiment with other fillings of fruit, seafood, etc.)

PALACSINTA (HUNGARIAN DESSERT PANCAKES)

Representative **Ted Weiss**—*New York*

I was born in Hungary and emigrated to the United States as a young boy. Palacsinta is a traditional Hungarian dessert and an old family recipe. It is a favorite of my family as well as the Eastern European community in the district I represent.

1 cup (4 ounces) all-purpose white
    flour
1 egg
1 cup milk
    Pinch salt
½ cup seltzer or club soda
    Vegetable oil for cooking
    Jam or preserves (for garnish)
    Confectioners' sugar (for garnish)

Sift flour into a bowl. Add egg, milk and salt. Beat gently until smooth. Add seltzer or club soda. Beat batter with wooden spoon until smooth. Put batter in cool place and allow it to rest for 10 to 15 minutes.

Pour some oil into skillet and allow it to get very hot, but not smoking. Pour in a small amount of batter, thinly covering bottom of pan. Cook in hot oil until crisp. Turn pancake over and fry on other side. Add oil as necessary. If batter begins to thicken, thin it with small amount of seltzer.

Spread pancakes with your favorite jam or preserves. They may be rolled up or folded in half. Sprinkle pancakes with powdered sugar and serve while still warm.

This recipe should produce 12 paper-thin pancakes.

NALESZ NIKI
(POLISH-STYLE CREPES)

Representative **Paul E. Kanjorski**—*Pennsylvania*
Recipe from: Mrs. Kanjorski

Nalesz Niki is a Polish version of the French crepe. The Kanjorski family enjoys this dish when entertaining or as a special breakfast treat. It may be served with or without the accompanying blueberry sauce.

    1 cup all-purpose white flour
 1½ cup milk
    2 eggs
    1 tablespoon vegetable oil
  ¼ teaspoon salt
      Granulated sugar, marmalade, or
        blueberry sauce (below)
Blueberry Sauce
 2½ cups fresh or frozen blueberries,
        divided
  ½ cup water
  ¾ cup granulated sugar
    2 tablespoons water
    2 tablespoons cornstarch
    2 tablespoons lemon juice
  Garnish
      Whipped cream (optional)

To prepare crepes, beat together flour, milk, eggs, oil and salt with a wire whisk until smooth. Lightly grease, then heat a nonstick skillet or crepe pan. Remove from heat. Immediately pour ½ cup batter into pan, tilting to spread evenly. Return to heat. Cook on one side until lightly set, then turn with a long knife-like spatula. Cook 30 seconds longer. Repeat until all batter is used.

While still warm, sprinkle each crepe with granulated sugar or spread with marmalade, then roll up. May be served in this way without sauce.

To prepare blueberry sauce, combine 1 cup blueberries with ½ cup water. Bring to boil in medium-sized saucepan. Reduce heat and simmer 2 minutes. Add sugar and stir to dissolve. Mix remaining water with cornstarch. Gradually add to blueberry mixture. Cook, stirring constantly, until mixture has thickened. Remove from heat. Stir in remaining blueberries. Stir in lemon juice. Spoon sauce over Nalesz Niki and, if desired, garnish with whipped cream.

Chapter 9

Cakes & Cookies

CHOCOLATE CREAM CHEESE LAYER CAKE WITH ICING

Senator **Joe Biden**—*Delaware*
Recipe from: Jill Biden

This is our family's favorite chocolate cake recipe.

2 3-ounce packages cream cheese, softened
½ cup butter or margarine, softened
1 teaspoon vanilla extract
6½ cups (1½ pounds) sifted confectioners' sugar
⅓ cup milk, room temperature
4 1-ounce squares unsweetened chocolate, melted and cooled
¼ cup butter or margarine, softened
3 eggs
2¼ cups all-purpose white flour
1 teaspoon baking powder
1 teaspoon baking soda
1 teaspoon salt
1¼ cups milk

Cream together cream cheese, ½ cup butter, and vanilla. Alternately beat in sugar and ⅓ cup milk. Blend in chocolate. Remove 2 cups of batter (which will be used as frosting); cover and refrigerate. Cream together remaining chocolate mixture and ¼ cup butter. Add eggs, beating well. Stir together dry ingredients. Beat into creamed mixture alternately with 1¼ cups milk. Turn into 2 greased and floured 9-inch cake pans. Bake in preheated 350-degree oven for 30 minutes. Cool in pans for 10 minutes. Remove, cool on racks. Remove frosting from refrigerator 15 minutes before frosting cake.

DARK CHOCOLATE CAKE

Representative **Matthew F. McHugh**—*New York*

1½ cups all-purpose white flour
3 tablespoons unsweetened cocoa
  powder
1 tablespoon baking soda
1 cup granulated sugar
½ teaspoon salt
⅓ cup vegetable oil
1 tablespoon vinegar
1 teaspoon vanilla extract
1 cup cold water

Sift together dry ingredients into a large bowl. Stir together remaining ingredients. Combine liquid mixture with dry ingredients until well blended.

Bake batter in ungreased 8-inch square pan in preheated 350-degree oven for 30 to 35 minutes.

MAGGIE CAKE

Senator **David Boren**—*Oklahoma*

This recipe is named for Maggie Prather of Stratford, Oklahoma, who is a life-long friend of the A. H. Shi family. The Shis are the parents of my wife, Molly Shi Boren. This has been a family favorite for many years.

1 cup butter
2½ cups granulated sugar
5 eggs, separated
1 cup commercial buttermilk
5 teaspoons coffee
3 cups all-purpose white flour
1 teaspoon baking powder
1 teaspoon baking soda
4 teaspoons unsweetened cocoa powder
1 teaspoon salt
2 teaspoons vanilla extract

Icing

3 teaspoons coffee
1 egg
½ cup butter
2 teaspoons unsweetened cocoa powder
1 teaspoon vanilla extract
Dash salt
1 pound confectioners sugar
Cream
Pecans for garnish

To prepare cake, beat together butter and sugar. Beat egg yolks, buttermilk and coffee into creamed mixture. Stir together dry ingredients. Stir into liquid mixture. Stir vanilla into batter. Beat egg whites until stiff. Fold egg whites into batter. Divide batter among 5 greased pans and bake in preheated 350-degree oven for 15 to 20 minutes.

To prepare icing, put all ingredients except sugar, cream and pecans into mixing bowl. Start beating, gradually adding sugar, and a bit of cream if needed until spreading consistency is obtained. Ice cake and decorate with pecans.

NAMELESS CAKE

Senator **Dennis DeConcini**—*Arizona*

This cake is one that the DeConcini family traditionally uses for birthdays. It was discovered by the senator's mother, Ora, about 25 years ago in a magazine. The cake was part of a contest whereby you tried the recipe and submitted a name for the cake. Needless to say, since the cake is still nameless, she never learned who had won the contest or what the cake was named.
—Mrs. DeConcini

¾ cup shortening
1½ cups granulated sugar
3 eggs, well beaten
1¾ cups sifted all-purpose white flour
½ teaspoon baking soda
½ teaspoon salt
¾ teaspoon ground nutmeg
1 teaspoon ground cinnamon
3 tablespoons unsweetened cocoa powder
¾ cup commercial buttermilk
1 teaspoon vanilla extract
1 teaspoon lemon extract
½ cup pecans (chopped and toasted)

Icing
6 tablespoons butter
1 egg yolk
3 cups confectioners' sugar
1½ tablespoons unsweetened cocoa powder
1 teaspoon ground cinnamon
1½ tablespoons hot coffee (or more as needed)

To prepare cake, cream shortening and add sugar gradually. Cream thoroughly. Mix in eggs. Sift flour and all other dry ingredients together. Add to creamed mixture, alternately with buttermilk. Add extracts and nuts. Pour into well-greased and floured 8- or 9-inch layer cake pans; or bake in cupcake tins. Bake for 30 minutes in preheated 350-degree oven.

To prepare icing, cream butter. Blend in egg yolk. Sift sugar, cocoa and cinnamon together. Add to creamed mixture, alternately with hot coffee. Beat until smooth. If necessary, add a few more tablespoons coffee until icing spreads easily.

SOUR CREAM CAKE

Representative **Lee Hamilton**—*Indiana*

2 sticks margarine
2 cups granulated sugar
2 eggs
2 cups sifted cake flour
1 teaspoon baking powder
1 teaspoon vanilla extract
1 8-ounce carton commercial sour
   cream

Topping
1 teaspoon ground cinnamon
1 tablespoon granulated sugar
½ cup chopped pecans

Cream together margarine and sugar. Thoroughly beat in eggs one at a time. Stir together flour and baking powder. Beat into creamed mixture. Add vanilla and sour cream and mix well. To prepare topping, stir together all ingredients.

Grease bundt pan well and sprinkle half of topping in bottom and around sides of pan. Fold other half of topping into cake mixture and pour mixture into pan. Bake in preheated 325-degree oven for 1 hour. Do not open oven door while baking. Turn cake on to a plate immediately after removing from oven; lift off pan.

Cakes & Cookies

JELLO CAKE SUPREME

Representative **Robert C. Smith**—*New Hampshire*

An often requested recipe. Super-easy crowd pleaser!

1 18½-ounce package yellow cake mix
1 3-ounce package lemon gelatin
¾ cup water
¾ cup vegetable oil
4 eggs

Sauce
1 cup orange juice
2 tablespoons lemon juice
2 cups confectioners' sugar
2 tablespoons butter

To serve:
Whipped cream for garnish
Thin lemon slices for garnish

Beat together all cake ingredients until smooth. Pour into *ungreased* 10 x 13-inch pan. Bake 35 minutes in preheated 350-degree oven. When done, prick all over with 2-pronged fork (try not to go all the way to bottom) and pour sauce over cake while still hot.

To prepare sauce, combine all ingredients in saucepan. Heat slightly to melt butter. Drizzle over cake. Refrigerate cake several hours before serving. Serve with dollop of whipped cream and thin slice of lemon.

Makes 16 servings.

FRUIT COCKTAIL CAKE

Senator **Daniel Inouye**—*Hawaii*
Recipe from: Maggie Inouye

This is a variation of a recipe from Mrs. Thomas J. McCabe of Honolulu.

1   18½-ounce package banana cake mix
1   3¾-ounce package banana instant pudding mix
1   16-ounce can fruit cocktail, drained and syrup reserved
1   cup shredded coconut
4   eggs, at room temperature
¼   cup vegetable oil
½   cup brown sugar, packed
½   cup chopped macadamia nuts

Glaze and garnish
½   cup butter
⅓   cup granulated sugar
½   cup evaporated milk (small can)
1   teaspoon vanilla extract
1   cup shredded coconut for garnish

Mix together cake mix, pudding mix, fruit cocktail syrup, shredded coconut, eggs and oil. Beat for 2 minutes. Fold in fruit cocktail. Pour into greased 9 x 13-inch or 2 8 x 8-inch pans. Mix together brown sugar and nuts. Sprinkle over cake batter. Bake in preheated 325-degree oven for 45 minutes. Do not underbake. Cool for 15 minutes.

Meanwhile, prepare glaze by combining butter, granulated sugar, evaporated milk and vanilla in saucepan. Bring ingredients to a boil. Simmer for 2 minutes. Sprinkle 1 cup coconut over cake while hot. Spoon hot glaze over coconut.

RUM CAKE

Representative **Ed Jones**—*Tennessee*
Recipe from: Llewellyn Jones

½ cup chopped pecans
1 18½-ounce package yellow cake mix
1 3¾-ounce package vanilla instant
     pudding mix
½ cup light rum
½ cup milk
½ cup vegetable oil
4 eggs
Glaze
1 cup granulated sugar
1 stick butter or margarine
¼ cup rum
¼ cup water

To prepare cake, grease and flour a bundt pan or tube pan. Crumble nuts into bottom of pan. Place cake mix and pudding mix in large mixing bowl. Add rum, milk, oil and eggs. Mix for 2 minutes. Pour batter into cake pan and bake in preheated 325-degree oven for 50 to 60 minutes. Remove cake from oven and immediately pour hot rum glaze over it. This will cause cake to settle. Cool cake before removing to serving plate.

To prepare glaze, combine ingredients and boil about 5 minutes until slightly thickened. Rum Cake can be frozen.

Makes 12 servings.

GRANDMOTHER'S APPLESAUCE CAKE

Representative **Cooper Evans**—*Iowa*
Recipe from: Jean Evans

A childhood memory that seems almost legendary to me now springs from the gathering of our large family for picnic dinner on every Fourth of July. Our marvelous menu seldom varied—baked beans, ham, potato salad and so on—and dessert lasted all afternoon.

Dessert traditionally was berry pie and cherry pie, but those summer beauties shared popularity with Grandmother's Applesauce Cake . . . and this is the recipe that most of us have copied in the back of our cookbooks. Really, it needs no topping. However, fluffy boiled icing is very good (joyfully sticky); vanilla-flavored butter and powdered sugar spread is richly old-fashioned. And if your group prepares some homemade ice cream, you won't forget the combination.

1 cup granulated sugar
½ cup shortening
2 eggs, slightly beaten
1 cup unsweetened applesauce
1¾ cups all-purpose white flour
1 teaspoon baking soda
¼ teaspoon ground cloves
¼ teaspoon ground cinnamon
¼ teaspoon ground nutmeg
1 cup raisins (boiled for 2 or 3 minutes and drained well)
1 cup chopped black walnuts (or others you may have)

Cream sugar and shortening. Add eggs, then applesauce. Sift together dry ingredients. Stir raisins and nuts into flour mixture. Add flour mixture to creamed ingredients. Spread batter in greased and floured 9 x 13-inch pan. Bake in preheated 350-degree oven for 35 to 40 minutes.

APPLE CAKE

Representative **Claudine Schneider**—*Rhode Island*

1½ cups vegetable oil
2 cups granulated sugar
2 teaspoons baking soda
2 teaspoons salt
2 teaspoons vanilla extract
½ cup shredded or grated coconut
3 cups finely chopped apples
1 cup raisins
1 cup chopped walnuts
3 cups unsifted all-purpose white flour

Preheat oven to 325 degrees. Grease and flour a 9 x 13-inch baking pan. Stir together oil, sugar, soda, salt and vanilla. Stir in coconut, apples, raisins and walnuts until well distributed. Add flour and stir until mixed. Bake at 325 degrees for about 30 minutes or until center springs back to touch.

CARROT CAKE

Senator **Carl Levin**—*Michigan*

This recipe is designed for a food processor; however, it can be adapted to a mixer.

1 cup all-purpose white flour
¾ cup granulated sugar
1 teaspoon baking powder
¾ teaspoon baking soda
½ teaspoon ground cinnamon
½ teaspoon salt
2 eggs
⅝ cup vegetable oil
1 cup grated carrots
Small can crushed pineapple, drained
½ cup coarsely chopped walnuts
Frosting
6 tablespoons butter
1 3-ounce package cream cheese
½ teaspoon vanilla extract
3 heaping tablespoons confectioners' sugar

To prepare cake, put all dry ingredients in food processor bowl and mix 5 to 10 seconds. Add eggs and oil and mix 30 seconds; mixture will be very thick. Add carrots and pineapple and process thoroughly. Add nuts and process only to distribute. Bake in greased pan in preheated 350-degree oven about 1 hour.

To prepare frosting, process butter, cheese and vanilla for about 20 seconds. Add sugar and continue mixing. When cake is cold, pat frosting all over.

GERMAN COFFEE CAKE

Representative **Richard T. Schulze**—*Pennsylvania*

Whenever Nancy would ask the children what kind of cake they wanted her to bake for their birthday, they would always say this one. So I guess you could call this the traditional Schulze birthday cake.

1 cup butter or margarine
2 cups granulated sugar
3 cups all-purpose white flour
2 teaspoons baking soda
½ teaspoon salt
4 egg yolks, well beaten
2 cups commercial sour cream
2 teaspoons vanilla extract
4 egg whites, stiffly beaten
Streusel
¾ cup shredded or grated coconut
1 teaspoon ground cinnamon
½ cup granulated sugar

Cream together butter and sugar. Sift together flour, baking soda and salt. Add dry ingredients to shortening mixture. Gradually add beaten egg yolks, sour cream and vanilla. Gently fold in the stiffly beaten egg whites. In a separate bowl, mix together the coconut, cinnamon and ½ cup sugar.

Grease and flour a tube or bundt pan. Alternately pour layers of batter and sprinkle streusel into baking pan, beginning and ending with batter.

Bake in preheated 375-degree oven for about 60 minutes. Cool for 20 minutes before turning out onto a cake plate.

LEMON BARS

Vice President **George Bush**

For lemon lovers of America! This is a favorite of ours—we borrowed the recipe from my dear friend Antoinette Hatfield, wife of Senator Mark O. Hatfield.

Crust
- 1 cup butter or margarine
- 2 cups confectioners' sugar
- 2 cups all-purpose white flour

Filling
- 4 teaspoons lemon juice
- Grated rind of 2 lemons
- 4 eggs, well beaten
- 2 cups granulated sugar
- 1 teaspoon baking powder
- ¼ cup all-purpose white flour
- 1 cup shredded coconut (optional)

To prepare crust, thoroughly mix crust ingredients and spread out in greased 9 x 13-inch pan. Bake for 15 minutes in preheated 350-degree oven until very pale tan. Cool.

To prepare filling, thoroughly mix together all ingredients. Pour over crust and bake at 350 degrees for 25 minutes. Cool thoroughly and serve cut into small bars.

AMAZING CHOCOLATE BROWNIES

Representative **Dave McCurdy**—*Oklahoma*

The secret to these brownies is not to overcook them. When they are baked just right they are amazing . . . and the hit of many a staff meeting!

1 cup brown sugar, packed
1 cup granulated sugar
1 cup vegetable oil
2 teaspoons vanilla extract
4 eggs
2 cups all-purpose white flour
1 teaspoon baking powder
2 tablespoons unsweetened cocoa powder
2 1-ounce squares melted semisweet chocolate
1 6-ounce package (1 cup) semisweet chocolate chips

Mix ingredients in order listed with a fork. Pour into greased 9 x 13-inch baking pan. Bake in preheated 350-degree oven for 25 to 30 minutes, or until done. (Baking time may vary; the middle should be set but not dry.)

LILLIAN'S ROCKY ROAD FUDGE BARS

Representative **George Darden**—*Georgia*

Bottom layer
- ½ cup butter or margarine
- 1 1-ounce square unsweetened chocolate
- 1 cup granulated sugar
- 1 cup all-purpose white flour
- ½ to 1 cup chopped nuts
- 1 teaspoon baking powder
- 1 teaspoon vanilla extract
- 2 eggs

Filling
- 1 8-ounce package cream cheese, softened (reserve 2 ounces for top layer)
- ½ cup granulated sugar
- 2 tablespoons all-purpose white flour
- ¼ cup butter or margarine, softened
- 1 egg
- ½ teaspoon vanilla extract
- ¼ cup chopped nuts
- 1 6-ounce package (1 cup) semisweet chocolate pieces (optional)
- 3 cups miniature marshmallows

Top layer
- ¼ cup butter or margarine
- 1 1-ounce square unsweetened chocolate
- Remaining 2 ounces cream cheese
- ¼ cup milk
- 1 pound (3 cups) confectioners' sugar
- 1 teaspoon vanilla extract

Preheat oven to 350 degrees. Grease and flour 9 x 13-inch pan. To prepare bottom layer, in large saucepan over low heat, melt ½ cup butter and 1 ounce chocolate. Add remaining ingredients. Mix well. Spread in prepared pan.

To prepare filling, in small bowl, combine 6 ounces cream cheese with remaining filling ingredients except nuts, chocolate chips and marshmallows. Blend until smooth and fluffy. Stir in nuts. Spread mixture over bottom layer. If desired, sprinkle with chocolate pieces. Bake in preheated 350-degree oven for 25 to 35 minutes until toothpick inserted in center comes out clean. Sprinkle with marshmallows and bake 2 minutes longer.

To prepare top layer, in large saucepan over low heat, melt butter, chocolate, remaining 2 ounces cream cheese and milk. Stir in confectioners' sugar and vanilla until smooth. Immediately pour over marshmallows and swirl together. Store in refrigerator. Cut into small bars before serving.

Makes 3 dozen bars.

CHOCOLATE COOKIES

Senator **Howell Heflin**—*Alabama*

1 **12-ounce package semisweet chocolate chips**
1 **14-ounce can sweetened condensed milk (fresh)**
4 **tablespoons (½ stick) butter**
1 **cup sifted all-purpose white flour**
¾ **cup chopped pecans**
1 **teaspoon vanilla extract**

Combine chocolate chips, condensed milk, and butter in double boiler over simmering water. Heat until ingredients are melted. Cool chocolate mixture slightly. Add flour, pecans and vanilla. Mix thoroughly. Drop by half-teaspoonfuls on ungreased cookie sheet. Bake for 7 minutes *only* in preheated 350-degree oven.

Makes about 90 cookies.

POLVORONES

Representative **Henry B. Gonzalez**—*Texas*

Polvorones are delightful, melt-in-the-mouth, small Mexican cookies which are particularly popular around Christmas time in the southwest part of the United States as well as in Mexico.

4½ cups sifted all-purpose white flour
¾ cup granulated sugar
2 teaspoons ground cinnamon
⅔ cup pure lard
2 eggs, lightly beaten

Coating mixture

1 cup granulated sugar
1½ teaspoons ground cinnamon

Mix flour, sugar and cinnamon in a large bowl. Add lard to dry ingredients and blend well. Add eggs and knead by hand in bowl until ingredients are blended and dough is smooth. Pinch off small pieces of dough and roll into small balls about the size of a nickel. Place on ungreased baking sheet and bake about 10 to 12 minutes, or until golden brown. Remove sheets from oven to wire racks and cool slightly. Stir together sugar and cinnamon coating mixture. Using a spatula, remove 2 or 3 cookies at a time from baking sheet. Gently place on platter containing cinnamon and sugar mixture. Coat generously with mixture; remove cookies to serving platter using slotted spoon.

Makes 6 to 7 dozen.

DATE-FILLED COOKIES

Senator **James Abdnor**—*South Dakota*
Recipe from: Mary Wehby Abdnor
(Senator Abdnor's mother)

Filling
>   1 **pound dates, pitted and chopped**
>   **(raisins may be substituted)**
> ½ **cup granulated sugar**
> ½ **cup water**
>   1 **cup chopped nuts**

Dough
>   1 **cup butter or shortening**
>   1 **cup granulated sugar**
>   1 **cup brown sugar, packed**
>   3 **eggs**
>   4 **cups all-purpose white flour**
>   1 **teaspoon baking soda**
>   1 **teaspoon ground cinnamon**
> ¼ **teaspoon salt**
>   1 **teaspoon vanilla extract**

To prepare filling, combine dates, sugar, and water.
Cook until a thick paste is formed, stirring
occasionally. Add nuts and set aside to cool before
using.

To prepare dough, cream butter, sugar and brown
sugar. Then add beaten eggs. Sift together flour, soda,
cinnamon and salt. Add to creamed mixture. Stir in
vanilla. If dough seems soft, chill slightly, then roll
out ½-inch thick. Spread with date filling and roll like
a jelly roll. Refrigerate several hours and preferably
overnight. Slice cookies and bake 10 to 15 minutes in
preheated 350-degree oven.

Makes 4 dozen cookies.

Chapter 10

Pies & Desserts

Pies

Cheesecakes

Puddings

Sherbet

Flan

PUMPKIN PECAN PIE

President **Ronald Reagan**
Recipe from: Nancy Reagan

  4 **eggs, slightly beaten**
  2 **cups canned or mashed cooked**
      pumpkin
  1 **cup granulated sugar**
  ½ **cup dark corn syrup**
  1 **teaspoon vanilla extract**
  ½ **teaspoon ground cinnamon**
  ¼ **teaspoon salt**
  1 **unbaked 9-inch pastry shell**
  1 **cup chopped pecans**

Combine all ingredients, except pecans. Pour into pie shell. Top with pecans. Bake in preheated 350-degree oven for 40 minutes, or until set.

GEORGIA PECAN PIE

Senator **Sam Nunn**—*Georgia*

1¼ cups granulated sugar
½ cup light corn syrup
¼ cup butter or margarine
3 eggs, slightly beaten
1 cup coarsely chopped pecans
1 teaspoon vanilla extract
1 unbaked 9-inch pastry shell

Preheat oven to 350 degrees. Combine sugar, syrup, and butter in 2-quart saucepan. Bring to boil on high, stirring constantly until butter is melted. Remove from stove and gradually add hot syrup to eggs, stirring constantly. Add pecans to mixture and cool to lukewarm. Add vanilla. Pour into pie shell and bake at 350 degrees for 40 to 45 minutes.

Makes 6 to 8 servings.

PECAN-RITZ PIE

Representative **Richard Ray**—*Georgia*

20 Ritz crackers
1 teaspoon baking powder
1 teaspoon vanilla extract
1 cup chopped pecans
3 egg whites
1 cup granulated sugar
1 cup whipped cream for garnish
   Cherries or chocolate chips for
   garnish

Crush crackers fine in a bowl. Add baking powder, vanilla and pecans. Beat egg whites, gradually adding sugar, until stiff. Fold whites into cracker mixture. Pour mixture into a greased 9-inch pie plate. (The mixture forms its own crust.) Bake for 30 minutes in preheated 350-degree oven. Cool and top with whipped cream and a cherry or use chocolate chips.

ORANGE-PECAN PIE

Representative **E. (Kika) de la Garza**—*Texas*

Several drops vanilla extract
1 **cup light corn syrup**
¼ **cup granulated sugar**
¼ **cup melted butter**
1 **cup chopped Texas pecans**
1 **tablespoon Texas orange juice**
1 **tablespoon grated Texas orange rind**
3 **eggs, beaten**
½ **teaspoon salt**
1 **unbaked 9-inch pastry shell**

Combine all filling ingredients in a medium-sized mixing bowl and mix well. Pour into pastry shell. Bake in preheated 350-degree oven for 45 minutes.

KENTUCKY PIE

Senator **Wendell Ford**—*Kentucky*

*The following recipe has
been a Ford family favorite
for many years.*

1 cup granulated sugar
½ cup all-purpose white flour
½ cup (1 stick) melted butter or
  margarine
2 eggs, slightly beaten
1 6-ounce package semisweet
  chocolate chips
1 cup pecans, chopped
1 teaspoon vanilla extract
1 9-inch unbaked pie shell

Mix together sugar and flour. Add melted butter and
blend well. Stir in eggs, chocolate chips, nuts and
vanilla. Pour mixture into pie shell. Bake in
preheated 325-degree oven 1 hour or until golden
brown.

Makes 6 to 8 very rich servings.

ICE BOX PIE

Senator **Nancy Landon Kassebaum**—*Kansas*

3 1-ounce squares semisweet chocolate
⅓ stick butter
2 cups Rice Krispies cereal
Ice cream such as coffee crunch
Grated chocolate for garnish

Melt chocolate with butter. Stir in cereal until well mixed. Grease a 10-inch pie plate and press mixed ingredients into it. Fill with ice cream. Top with grated chocolate. Freeze. Take out of freezer about ½ hour before serving so pie can soften slightly.

LOUISIANA SWEET POTATO PIE WITH SOUR CREAM TOPPING

Senator **James T. Broyhill**—*North Carolina*

This recipe was a favorite of my late friend, Congressman Gillis Long, who used to say: "Baked, boiled, fried, candied or cooked in a pie, Louisiana yams are extraordinary!" The sour cream is especially delicious with this pie. Enjoy!

2 cups cooked, mashed sweet potatoes
1 cup brown sugar, packed
1 cup light cream
½ cup milk
3 eggs
½ teaspoon salt
1 teaspoon ground cinnamon
1 teaspoon ground nutmeg
½ teaspoon ground ginger
1 unbaked 9-inch pastry shell
Topping
2 cups commercial sour cream
½ cup confectioners' sugar
½ teaspoon vanilla extract

In large mixing bowl, thoroughly combine sweet potatoes, sugar, cream, milk, eggs, salt, cinnamon, nutmeg and ginger. Pour into pastry shell. Bake in preheated 350-degree oven for 1 hour, or until knife inserted in center comes out clean. Cool thoroughly.

To prepare topping: Mix sour cream, sugar and vanilla. Serve with cooled pie.

DELLUMS'
SWEET POTATO PIE

Representative **Ron Dellums**—*California*

This Dellums family favorite is of Afro-American origin. This Southern dish is thought to be tastier than traditional pumpkin pie and is served at Thanksgiving and Christmas and on the Fourth of July.

1 2-pound can yams, drained (or 5 cups fresh cooked yams)
Dash ground cinnamon
Dash ground nutmeg
⅓ cup light brown sugar, packed
1⅓ cups granulated sugar
½ teaspoon vanilla extract
¼ teaspoon almond extract
1⅓ sticks butter
3 eggs, beaten
1 12-ounce can evaporated milk, or half-and-half
1 unbaked 9-inch pastry shell

Mash drained yams with a masher or fork. Dust yams with cinnamon and nutmeg. Add brown sugar and granulated sugar. Stir in vanilla and almond extracts. Melt butter and stir into yam mixture. Add beaten eggs, then milk. Blend ingredients thoroughly; mixture will look soupy. On a low flame cook and stir until ingredients are well blended. Mix well with blender. Pour into 9-inch unbaked pie shell. Bake pie in preheated 350-degree oven for 35 to 40 minutes or until crust is golden brown and filling springs back to touch.

CHOCOLATE CHIP PIE

Representative **Byron L. Dorgan**—*North Dakota*

 10 graham crackers, rolled into
    fine crumbs
  2 tablespoons butter
 30 marshmallows
½ to ¾ cup milk
  2 squares unsweetened chocolate, very
    finely grated
  1 cup heavy cream, whipped until firm
    Maraschino cherries or chocolate
    sprinkles for garnish

Mix together graham cracker crumbs and butter.
Press very firmly into bottom and sides of pie plate.

Melt marshmallows with milk in double boiler over
simmering water. Cool. Beat well. Fold grated
chocolate into whipped cream; then fold this mixture
into marshmallow mixture. Pour into graham cracker
crust. Top with cherries or chocolate sprinkles, if
desired. Chill in refrigerator overnight or at least 3
hours before serving.

BROWN SUGAR APPLE PIE

Senator **Steven D. Symms**—*Idaho*

Apple pie, long the symbol of basic American ideals, has been disappearing from the American table just as many of those ideals have been disappearing from the American government. (Can it be that the shortage of apple pie in the diets of congressmen has caused the rapid growth of government?)

2½ cups all-purpose white flour
1 teaspoon salt
¾ cup shortening
¼ cup cold water
3 heaping cups thinly sliced tart apples
1½ cups brown sugar, packed
½ teaspoon ground cinnamon
½ teaspoon ground nutmeg
⅓ cup butter

To make pie crust: Combine flour and salt. Cut in shortening. Sprinkle water over mixture and mix lightly with a fork. Gather dough into a ball and chill. Then roll out bottom and top crusts.

Fill bottom shell with apples. Sprinkle with sugar and spices. Cut generous chips of butter over all. Add top crust; seal edges and flute. Prick crust with fork. Bake in preheated 375-degree oven for 60 minutes.

PEACH PIE

Representative **Beverly Byron**—*Maryland*

Pastry
>   2 cups all-purpose white flour
>   ½ teaspoon salt
>   ⅔ cup butter
>   Ice water

Filling
>   6 to 8 fresh, peeled and pitted peaches, sliced
>   ¼ cup all-purpose white flour
>   1 cup granulated sugar
>   1 cup heavy cream
>   Dash ground nutmeg
>   Dash ground cinnamon

To prepare pastry: Sift together flour and salt. Cut in butter. Gradually add enough water to press dough into a firm ball. Chill dough, then divide in two portions, one slightly larger than the other. Roll out larger portion to form shell. Reserve other portion for lattice top.

Lay peach slices in pastry shell. Mix together remaining filling ingredients. Pour over peaches. Add lattice top. Bake in preheated 350-degree oven for 1 to 1½ hours.

KEY LIME PIE

Representative **Charles E. Bennett**—*Florida*

The following Key lime pie recipe is one of my favorites and a special recipe from the Sunshine State of Florida.

1⅓ **cups graham cracker crumbs**
½ **stick butter, melted**
3 **eggs, separated**
1 **14-ounce can sweetened condensed milk**
¾ **cup fresh Key lime juice**
6 **tablespoons granulated sugar**
1 **teaspoon vanilla extract**

Mix crumbs and butter and press onto sides and bottom of 9-inch pie plate. Beat egg yolks until light. Beat in condensed milk and lime juice, beating until mixture is thick. Pour into pie shell. Beat egg whites until they hold stiff peaks. Beat in sugar, a tablespoon at a time, until mixture is stiff and glossy. Beat in vanilla. Spread meringue on pie top, sealing edges to crust. Bake in preheated 425-degree oven for 5 to 7 minutes. Chill before serving.

Makes 6 servings.

FROZEN RASPBERRY PIE

Representative **Mary Rose Oakar**—*Ohio*

1 10-ounce package frozen raspberries
   including syrup, thawed
2 egg whites
1 cup granulated sugar
1 cup heavy cream
1 teaspoon almond extract
1 9-inch pie shell (either baked pastry
   or graham cracker)
   Slivered almonds for garnish

Beat raspberries and egg whites for 15 minutes, gradually adding sugar. Beat together cream and almond extract until cream is stiff. Fold together egg white and cream mixtures. Pour into shell. Top with almonds. Cover and freeze.

CHEESECAKE

Senator **Dan Quayle**—*Indiana*

Crust
> 1 cup graham cracker crumbs
> 3 teaspoons granulated sugar
> 3 tablespoons melted butter

Filling
> 4 eggs, well beaten
> 1 cup granulated sugar
> 1 teaspoon vanilla extract
> 3 8-ounce packages cream cheese, softened

Topping
> 1 cup commercial sour cream
> 2 tablespoons granulated sugar
> ½ teaspoon vanilla extract

To prepare crust: Mix ingredients and press into 9-inch springform pan.

To prepare filling: Mix eggs, sugar, vanilla and cream cheese with electric mixer until completely smooth. Pour over crust.

Bake in preheated 375-degree oven for 30 minutes. Remove from oven and cool 10 minutes. Meanwhile, increase heat to 475 degrees. Also, prepare topping by stirring together sour cream, sugar and vanilla. Spoon over cheesecake. Return cheesecake to oven and bake 5 minutes longer. Cool cheesecake thoroughly before serving.

LYNNE'S CHEESECAKE FOR RUDY

Senator **Rudy Boschwitz**—*Minnesota*

Rudy loves cheesecake and is, in his own words, "a great cheesecake tester." This is the best he's found. He's blessed with a metabolism that consumes calories. The recipe originally came to him from a staff person in the Senate.
—Mrs. Boschwitz

Pastry

- 1 **cup all-purpose white flour**
- ¼ **cup granulated sugar**
- 1 **stick cold, unsalted butter**
- 1 **large egg yolk, beaten**
- 1 **teaspoon vanilla extract**
- 1 **teaspoon grated lemon rind**

Filling

- 5 **8-ounce packages cream cheese, softened**
- 1¾ **cups granulated sugar**
- 3 **tablespoons all-purpose white flour**
- 1½ **teaspoons grated orange rind**
- 1½ **teaspoons grated lemon rind**
- ½ **teaspoon vanilla extract**
- 5 **eggs**
- 2 **egg yolks**
- ¼ **cup heavy cream**

To prepare pastry: Into a large bowl sift together flour and sugar. Add butter, cut into bits, and egg yolk. Add vanilla and grated lemon rind. Blend mixture until well combined (either in food processor or with pastry cutter). Form dough into two balls, one slightly larger than the other. Remove sides of a 9-inch springform pan; press smaller ball into bottom of pan.

Bake pastry in preheated 400-degree oven for 8 to 10 minutes or until lightly browned. Cool completely. Butter sides of pan, attach to bottom, and press remaining dough 1¾ inches up pan sides, pressing firmly but gently where sides join bottom. Set aside.

To prepare filling: Heat oven to 500 degrees. In large bowl, beat cream cheese, sugar, flour, orange and lemon rind, vanilla and 2 eggs until smooth. Continue beating, adding remaining eggs and yolks, one at a time, until blended. On low speed, blend in cream. Pour into pastry-lined pan. Bake 12 to 15 minutes. Reduce oven temperature to 200 degrees; bake 1 hour longer. Cool. Refrigerate overnight, or 12 to 24 hours. Loosen cake from side of pan; remove side, leaving cake on bottom of pan.

CHOCOLATE MELT-AWAY DESSERT

Representative **Dan Burton**—*Indiana*

Crust
- 1 cup all-purpose white flour
- ¼ cup confectioners' sugar
- 1 stick margarine
- ½ to ¾ cup chopped nuts

Filling
- 2 sticks margarine
- 2 cups confectionars' sugar
- 4 1-ounce squares unsweetened chocolate, melted
- 1 teaspoon vanilla extract
- 4 eggs

Topping and garnish
- 1 8-ounce carton nondairy topping (Cool Whip)
- Chocolate curls (optional)

To prepare crust: Mix together flour, sugar and margarine. Press into 9 x 13-inch pan. Sprinkle with nuts. Bake 15 minutes in preheated 350-degree oven.

Beat together all filling ingredients except eggs. Add eggs one at a time; beat 10 minutes. Spread over crust. Top with nondairy topping. Chill well. Garnish with chocolate curls, if desired. Cut into squares to serve.

HUNGARIAN RHAPSODY DESSERT

Representative **Tom Lantos**—*California*
Recipe from: Annette Lantos

Crust
- 1 **cup butter, melted**
- ½ **cup confectioners' sugar**
- 2 **cups all-purpose white flour**

Filling
- 1½ **cups butter or margarine**
- 1⅓ **cups sugar, divided**
- 8 **eggs, separated**
- 3 **teaspoons lemon juice *or* vanilla extract**
- ⅓ **cup all-purpose white flour**
- 2 **8-ounce packages cream cheese, softened**

To prepare crust: Mix melted butter, confectioners' sugar, and flour until blended. Pat into 9 x 13-inch flat ovenproof casserole. Bake for 20 minutes in preheated 350-degree oven.

To prepare filling: Cream together butter with 1 cup sugar. Add egg yolks, one at a time, beating well after each addition. Add lemon juice or vanilla. Add flour and cream cheese. Cream until smooth. Whip egg whites, gradually adding remaining ⅓ cup sugar. Fold into egg yolk mixture. Pour into crust. Bake in 350-degree oven 35 to 45 minutes. Dessert is done when knife inserted in thickest part comes out clean. Dust with confectioners' sugar. Cut into small squares. May be frozen.

Makes 18 to 22 servings.

CHOCOLATE ANGELFOOD DESSERT

Representative **Tom Tauke**—*Iowa*

2 packages German sweet chocolate
2 tablespoons water
4 eggs, separated
¼ teaspoon salt
1 teaspoon vanilla extract
2 cups whipped cream
1 angelfood cake

To serve:

Whipped cream for garnish
1 small package sliced almonds

Break chocolate bars in small squares; place in double boiler over simmering water. Add water and slowly heat until chocolate is melted. Beat egg yolks until frothy. Beat in salt and vanilla. Beat egg mixture into chocolate; set aside until cool.

Beat egg whites. Then fold into cooled chocolate mixture. Fold in whipped cream.

Slice cake into very thin slices. Place a layer in bottom of 9 x 13-inch pan. Spoon half of chocolate mixture on top. Repeat with layer of cake, layer of chocolate, continuing until chocolate is last layer.

Refrigerate for at least 5 hours before serving. Keeps well in refrigerator for several days. To serve dessert, cut in squares. Top with additional whipped cream and almond slices.

CUT A RIBBON CAKE

Senator **Mark O. Hatfield**—*Oregon*

Although called a cake, this is really a lemon charlotte dessert.

8 **eggs, separated**
2 **cups granulated sugar**
8 **teaspoons lemon juice**
2 **packages unflavored gelatin**
½ **cup cold water**
  Grated rind of 2 medium-sized lemons
2 **packages ladyfingers**
1 **cup whipped cream for garnish**
  Fresh strawberries or peaches for garnish

Combine egg yolks, sugar and lemon juice in top of double boiler over simmering water. Cook, stirring constantly, until thick. Dissolve gelatin in cold water. Remove mixture from stove, add lemon rind and dissolved gelatin. Cool to room temperature. Beat egg whites until stiff and peaked. Fold into cool yolk mixture.

Line a springform pan with single ladyfingers in an unbroken row around the sides and like spokes of a wheel in the bottom. Pour in lemon mixture and let set overnight in the refrigerator. Remove sides of pan and invert cake on a large plate. Decorate with whipped cream in spaces between ladyfingers (cream may be flavored with a little lemon rind) and fresh fruit. Tie a ribbon around the circumference of the cake to be cut by the guest of honor.

SEMOLINA CAKE

Representative **Gene Chappie**—*California*

> 1 **cup cream of wheat or semolina**
> 4 **cups milk**
> ⅓ to ½ **cup granulated sugar, or to taste**
> 3 to 4 **eggs**
> 1 **teaspoon vanilla extract**
> **Bread crumbs**
>
> **To serve:**
>
> **Brandy**

Combine cream of wheat with milk and cook, stirring frequently, for 20 minutes or until it sticks to a wooden spoon. Beat in sugar. Beat eggs, one at a time, into a small portion of semolina. Add mixture to rest of semolina. Stir in vanilla.

Grease and coat 8- or 9-inch round cake pan with bread crumbs. Pat cooked mixture evenly into pan. Bake in preheated 350-degree oven until a knife inserted in center comes out clean. Pour 2 jiggers of brandy on top and serve.

SANDBAKKELSE

Representative **Lee Hamilton**—*Indiana*

Sandbakkelse are crisp tart shells which are served filled with fresh fruit.

½ **cup butter**
½ **cup margarine**
1 **cup granulated sugar**
2 **eggs**
2 **teaspoons vanilla extract**
½ **teaspoon salt**
2¾ **cups all-purpose white flour**

Cream butter and margarine. Gradually add sugar. Add eggs and beat well. Add remaining ingredients and mix well. Press dough into individual greased and floured (or Teflon coated) sandbakkel tins to form thin, hollow shells.

Bake 10 minutes in preheated 350-degree oven until light brown. When done, place tins on a board upside down. Allow to cool and tap lightly on tins to remove shells.

Serve sandbakkelse with fresh fruit of your choice.

LEMON CREAM SHERBET

Senator **Robert T. Stafford**—*Vermont*
Recipe from: Mrs. Stafford

1 cup granulated sugar
1 cup light cream
   Grated rind and juice of 1 large
      lemon
1 cup whipped cream

Combine sugar and light cream in saucepan and heat just enough to dissolve sugar. Cool. Add lemon juice and rind. Fold in whipped cream. Pour into ice tray. Freeze to mush. Stir and refreeze.

PLUM DUFF

Representative **Nancy L. Johnson**—*Connecticut*

This recipe is a family favorite given to me by my mother-in-law. It is so popular with my own children that it has become a Christmas tradition.

2 **eggs**
½ **cup shortening (half margarine, half butter)**
1 **cup brown sugar, packed**
1 **cup pitted cooked prunes**
1 **cup all-purpose white flour**
1 **teaspoon baking soda**
  Pinch salt
1 **tablespoon milk**
To serve:
  Whipped cream or ice cream

Beat together eggs, shortening and sugar until creamed. Stir in prunes. Stir together flour, baking soda and salt until well blended. Gradually add dry ingredients to creamed mixture. Stir in milk.

Spoon mixture into 2 greased round 8-inch cake pans. Bake in preheated 375-degree oven for 15 to 20 minutes.

BAKLAVA

Representative **Olympia J. Snowe**—*Maine*

A Greek dessert, baklava was introduced to Greece in the sixth century by its Byzantine rulers, Emperor Justinian and Empress Theodora. Baklava is also known as the "sweet of a thouand layers."

1½ **pounds walnuts, chopped**
¾ **cup granulated sugar**
1 **teaspoon ground cinnamon**
    Grated rind of 1 orange
1 **pound (4 sticks) butter**
1 **pound phyllo dough (strudel leaves)**
Syrup
2 **cups water**
2 **cups granulated sugar**
½ **cup honey**
1 **cinnamon stick**
3 **lemon slices**

Mix nuts, sugar, cinnamon and orange rind well. Melt butter. Brush some butter over surface of 9 x 13-inch pan. Place layer of phyllo in pan, allowing ends to extend over pan. Brush with melted butter. Repeat with 4 sheets of phyllo. Sprinkle heavily with nut mixture, and continue to assemble: add one layer of phyllo, brush with melted butter, sprinkle heavily with nut mixture and continue until all ingredients are used. Be sure to reserve 4 sheets of phyllo for top (each to be brushed with butter). Brush top with remaining butter. Trim edges with sharp knife. Cut through top with diagonal lines to form diamond shapes. Bake in preheated 400-degree oven for 15 minutes. Lower temperature to 300 degrees and continue to bake for 40 minutes. Should be golden brown.

Meanwhile, prepare syrup by combining all ingredients and boiling for 10 minutes. Remove lemon slices and cinnamon. While baklava is still hot, cover with prepared syrup and let stand overnight before serving. Will keep in refrigerator for weeks or can be frozen. Baklava should rest for 24 hours before being removed from pan.

Makes 24 servings.

CARAMEL FLAN

Representative **Larry Combest**—*Texas*

½ cup granulated sugar
4 eggs, beaten
1 14-ounce can sweetened, condensed milk
2 condensed milk cans filled with water
1 teaspoon vanilla extract

Melt sugar in heavy saucepan over medium heat until caramelized (caramel color liquid results). Immediately pour into 6-cup ovenproof or gelatin mold, tipping back and forth to coat bottom of container. Beat eggs together with milk and water. Add vanilla. Do not beat more than 2 minutes. Pour mixture over cooled sugar in mold.

Place mold in another container that is half full of warm water. Bake, covered, for 1½ hours in preheated 350-degree oven. Continue to bake, uncovered, 30 minutes longer or until a toothpick inserted in the thickest part comes out clean. Cool flan thoroughly before serving. Serve unmolded on platter.

Pies & Desserts

CARAMEL BRIE

Representative
F. James Sensenbrenner, Jr.—*Wisconsin*

Caramel Brie, a savory-sweet combination that looks like a glistening cake, is a favorite of Cheryl Sensenbrenner's.

1 wheel Brie (60 percent butterfat), about 2.8 pounds
2 cups granulated sugar
½ cup water
12 to 16 walnut or pecan halves (optional)

Put Brie on a rack over large sheet of parchment paper or aluminum foil. Combine sugar and water in heavy saucepan and melt sugar, swirling pan from time to time. Do not stir. When mixture begins to boil, cover pan to allow condensation to drip back down and melt crystallized sugar on pan sides. Uncover pan after 3 to 5 minutes and continue cooking over high heat until sugar becomes deep golden color. The temperature of caramel should be hard crack, 300 degrees.

Immediately pour caramel over cheese to cover top evenly, allowing excess to drip down sides. (You may have to tilt wheel a little to spread caramel evenly.) Be very careful not to touch hot caramel. Press nuts around perimeter, if desired. Caramel will harden quickly. Serve within an hour. Present cheese with small cheese knives. The guests will have to crack through coating, but this is part of the fun of eating such an unusual treat.

Note: When working with melted sugar or caramel, always keep a bowl of ice water nearby. If you should burn yourself, plunge the burned area into the water.

Makes 38 servings.

"SON-OF-A-BITCH" IN A SACK (DESSERT PUDDING)

Senator **Alan K. Simpson**—*Wyoming*

This recipe was given to the Simpson family by a rough-hewn old cowboy from the Cody Country, who called it an "about" recipe—"about so much of this and about so much of that."

2 cups finely chopped suet
1 teaspoon salt
1 quart (4 cups) all-purpose white
    flour, divided
    Large handful of raisins
    Water to make a stiff dough

Sauce

1 egg
1 cup granulated sugar
    Butter, size of an egg
3 tablespoons hot water
2 ounces good brandy

Add suet and salt to ⅔ of flour. Add raisins and enough water to make a stiff dough. Mix and roll in remaining flour. Place dough in a small sugar sack and boil in pot of hot water for 1 hour.

To prepare sauce, beat egg. Add sugar, butter and hot water. Add brandy. Cook in a double boiler over simmering water until thickened. Serve as sauce for pudding.

Chapter 11

Potpourri

Beverages

Sauces

Relishes

Snacks

etc.

SOUTH CAROLINA CHICKEN BARBECUE SAUCE

Senator **Strom Thurmond**—*South Carolina*

1 **pound butter**
4 **cups (1 quart) apple cider vinegar**
1 **cup chicken broth**
2 **cups water**
1 **10-ounce bottle Worcestershire sauce**
1 **9-ounce jar mustard**
2 **cups chili sauce**
  Juice of 3 lemons
¾ **2-ounce bottle hot sauce**
½ **teaspoon ground red pepper**
1 **onion, minced**
¼ **teaspoon black pepper**
  Cornstarch (optional)

Melt butter and add vinegar, broth and water. When well combined, add other ingredients and cook until onion is tender. Thicken with cornstarch stirred into a little cold water, as needed. Sauce is used as a basting sauce for grilling (parboiled) chicken. It may also be used to marinate chicken prior to grilling.

Note: Recipe may be halved or quartered, if desired.

FRESH TOMATO RELISH

Representative **Beverly Byron**—*Maryland*

6 tomatoes, peeled and diced
1 onion, peeled and minced
1 stalk celery, minced
1 medium-sized green pepper, minced
2 to 4 tablespoons chopped green chilies
3 tablespoons wine vinegar
½ teaspoon dried oregano leaves
1½ teaspoons cumin seeds, crushed
½ teaspoon ground cumin

Stir together all ingredients and chill 24 hours.

PEAR RELISH

Representative **J. J. Pickle**—*Texas*

My wife, Beryl, and I make this together. I peel and grind. She measures and cooks. This is Beryl's father's recipe.

8 large or 12 small pears (Keefer pears preferred)
3 medium-sized onions
5 red bell peppers
3 green bell peppers
3 cups white vinegar
3 cups granulated sugar
1 teaspoon celery seeds
1 teaspoon white mustard seeds
2 teaspoons salt
1 tablespoon cornstarch
Cold water

Pare and core pears. Grind together pears, onions and peppers in food grinder. Drain off most juice. Mix together vinegar, sugar, celery seeds, mustard seeds and salt. Pour over pear mixture and boil 20 minutes. Add cornstarch mixed with a little cold water. Simmer 15 more minutes. Pour in sterilized jars and seal.

Makes 6 pints.

RAW CRANBERRY RELISH
À LA NORVEGIENNE

Representative **Thomas E. Petri**—*Wisconsin*

This is an old Norwegian recipe. Norwegians use dwarf cranberries which we call lingonberries. This recipe is an adaptation of the original Norwegian dwarf cranberry recipe.

**1 quart (1 pound) raw cranberries,
fresh or frozen
1⅔ to 2 cups granulated sugar, or to taste
Grated rind of 1 orange**

Wash cranberries and place in large bowl with sugar and orange rind.

To prepare using a mixer: At low speed, beat mixture for 15 minutes. Let rest 30 minutes and beat again. Continue until sugar has dissolved completely.

To prepare by hand: Stir with wooden spoon for 5 minutes or more and give a vigorous turn for a few minutes whenever you feel like it until sugar dissolves. (It may take a day or two if you are lazy at stirring.)

Store relish in a jar (preferably screw-top jar), refrigerated. Relish will keep for weeks.

CRANBERRY FRAPPÉ

Senator **Mack Mattingly**—*Georgia*

Mrs. Mattingly's mother handed down this recipe. It can be used as a substitute for cranberry-orange relish at Thanksgiving or goes with any poultry or ham meal.

1 pound cranberries
2 cups water
1 orange
2 cups granulated sugar

Cook berries until soft in water. Sieve; then add grated rind and juice of orange. Add sugar, dissolving over heat. Freeze, beat, then refreeze.

BAKED FRUIT

Representative **Steny Hoyer**—*Maryland*

> 1 jar spiced apples
> 1 1-pound 4-ounce can sliced peaches
> 1 1-pound 4-ounce can pears
> 1 1-pound 4-ounce can pineapple
>   chunks
> 2 tablespoons all-purpose white flour
> ½ cup brown sugar, packed
> 1 stick butter
> 1 cup sherry

Drain fruits. Layer fruits in ovenproof casserole. Stir together flour and sugar. Add remaining ingredients and heat until butter melts. Pour over fruit. Refrigerate, covered, overnight. Bake in preheated 350-degree oven for 30 minutes.

Makes 6 to 8 servings.

COVE HOTEL PUNCH

Representative **Earl Hutto**—*Florida*

A number of years ago, the Cove Hotel was a popular place for people visiting "the world's most beautiful beaches" at Panama City, Florida. One of the favorites of both visitors and natives of the area who came to the hotel was the special punch served there. I hope you enjoy it as much as we do.

1 12-ounce can frozen orange juice concentrate, undiluted
3 6-ounce cans lemonade concentrate (reconstituted following can directions)
1 12-ounce can apricot nectar
1 46-ounce can pineapple juice
½ gallon orange sherbet
2 quarts ginger ale

Mix first 4 ingredients together and chill. Put ice cubes in bottom of bowl, along with sherbet. Add chilled juice mixture and pour ginger ale over all. Stir well.

Makes 40 servings.

FRESH PEACH DAIQUIRI

Representative **Richard Ray**—*Georgia*

3 to 5 ripe peaches (approximately), peeled,
        pitted and sliced
½ 6-ounce can frozen lemonade
       concentrate
1 6-ounce can ice-cold water
1 6-ounce can rum
1 tablespoon granulated sugar
8 to 10 ice cubes

Fill blender half full of sliced peaches. Add all
remaining ingredients. Blend quickly and serve
immediately. Enjoy!

FRENCH MINTS

Senator **Orrin G. Hatch**—*Utah*

4 1-ounce squares unsweetened
   chocolate*
1 cup soft butter
2 cups confectioners' sugar
4 eggs
1 teaspoon vanilla extract
1 teaspoon peppermint extract
  Nuts for garnish

Melt chocolate in double boiler over simmering water. Cool, set aside. Using electric beater, beat butter, gradually adding sugar (beat about 15 minutes). Add cooled melted chocolate. Beat 5 minutes more. Beat in eggs, one at a time. Mix in vanilla and peppermint extracts. Sprinkle chopped nuts on bottom of 24 paper cupcake liners. Fill half full and sprinkle nuts over top. Freeze mints for at least 3 hours.

Note: Can substitute 6-ounce package of semisweet chocolate chips for sweeter mints.

POPCORN BALLS

Representative **Neal Smith**—*Iowa*

> 2½ cups sorghum*
> ½ cup water
> ½ teaspoon salt
> ½ teaspoon apple cider vinegar
> 1 teaspoon vanilla extract
> 5 quarts popped popcorn

Mix sorghum, water, salt and vinegar and cook to a hard ball stage, 250 degrees. Add vanilla; pour mixture over popcorn and mix evenly. Let cool until sticky. Butter hands and form popcorn mixture into balls. Wrap in plastic to keep fresh.

Editor's note: If sorghum is unavailable, light molasses may be substituted.

INDEX BY RECIPE

AL'S FAVORITE CHILI . . . 57
AMAZING CHOCOLATE BROWNIES . . . 231
ANNIE GLENN'S HAM LOAF . . . 148
APPLE CAKE . . . 227
AUNT EDA'S NEVER FAIL CHEESE
    SOUFFLE . . . 95
AVOCADO AND SHRIMP IN BUTTER
    SAUCE . . . 16

BAKED CRAB IN SHELLS . . . 177
BAKED FRUIT . . . 277
BAKED GRITS WITH CHEESE . . . 88
BAKED LASAGNA WITH ITALIAN
    SAUCE . . . 116
BAKING POWDER BISCUITS . . . 202
BAKLAVA . . . 264
BANANA BREAD . . . 208
BEEF PEPPER STEAK . . . 129
BEEF SUKIYAKI . . . 131
BIG BEND BEAN DIP . . . 7
BILL'S MISSOURI CHILI . . . 60
BOURBON SWEET POTATOES . . . 79
BRATS 'N KRAUT . . . 149
BRAZOS RIVER STEW . . . 63
BROCCOLI OR SPINACH SOUP . . . 45
BROWN BREAD . . . 197
BROWN SUGAR APPLE PIE . . . 249
BUTTE PASTY . . . 121
BUTTERHORN ROLLS . . . 199

CALIENTE HOT DIP . . . 8
CAPE COD FISH CHOWDER . . . 51
CARAMEL BRIE . . . 267
CARAMEL FLAN . . . 266
CARROT CAKE . . . 228
CHALUPA CASSEROLE . . . 111
CHARLESTON SHE-CRAB SOUP . . . 44
CHEESECAKE . . . 253
CHICKEN BOG . . . 158
CHICKEN CROQUETTES . . . 172
CHICKEN FLORENTINE . . . 170
CHICKEN IN THE POT . . . 159
CHICKEN IN WINE . . . 167
CHICKEN SUPREME . . . 169

CHICKEN TUJAGUE . . . 102
CHICKEN-BROCCOLI CASSEROLE . . . 103
CHICKEN-PASTA SALAD . . . 28
CHILI CON 'CONTE' . . . 61
CHILIES AND CHEESE CASSEROLE . . . 97
CHILLED OLIVE-ASPARAGUS SOUP . . . 46
CHINESE CHICKEN WITH WALNUTS . . . 161
CHINESE SHREDDED CHICKEN SALAD . . . 26
CHINOOK SALMON CHOWDER . . . 50
CHOCOLATE ANGELFOOD DESSERT . . . 258
CHOCOLATE CHIP PIE . . . 248
CHOCOLATE COOKIES . . . 234
CHOCOLATE CREAM CHEESE LAYER CAKE
    WITH ICING . . . 218
CHOCOLATE MELT-AWAY DESSERT . . . 256
CITRUS LAMB . . . 152
COLD CARROT SOUP . . . 47
COMPANY POTATO CASSEROLE . . . 82
CONCH IN BUTTER SAUCE . . . 183
COPPER CARROT PENNIES . . . 73
COPPER COUNTRY PASTIES . . . 122
CORN PUDDING CASSEROLE . . . 80
CORNBREAD STUFFING . . . 89
COUNTRY CAPTAIN CHICKEN . . . 156
COVE HOTEL PUNCH . . . 278
CRANBERRY FRAPPÉ . . . 276
CREAMED ASPARAGUS . . . 68
CROCKPOT CORNISH HENS . . . 173
CUT A RIBBON CAKE . . . 259

DARK CHOCOLATE CAKE . . . 219
DATE-FILLED COOKIES . . . 236
DAVID EYRE PANCAKE . . . 212
DELLUMS' SWEET POTATO PIE . . . 247
DEVILED CRABMEAT CASSEROLE . . . 175
DUCK AND WILD RICE CASSEROLE . . . 104

EASY BUT RICH BEEF CASSEROLE . . . 106
ELECTION DAY CHILI . . . 58
ESKABECHI . . . 192

FETTUCCINE TOSS-UP . . . 85
FISH CHOWDER ON-THE-GRILL . . . 191
FLOWER POT BREAD . . . 198

FRANK AND NANCY'S CAESAR SALAD . . . 23
FRENCH MINTS . . . 280
FRESH PEACH DAIQUIRI . . . 279
FRESH STRAWBERRY SALAD . . . 36
FRESH TOMATO RELISH . . . 273
FRIED OKRA . . . 75
FROZEN RASPBERRY PIE . . . 252
FRUIT COCKTAIL CAKE . . . 224

GAZPACHO . . . 49
GEORGIA PECAN PIE . . . 241
GERMAN COFFEE CAKE . . . 229
GOOD NEIGHBOR CHICKEN . . . 168
GRANDMOTHER'S APPLESAUCE
    CAKE . . . 226
GREAT BARBECUED KENAI SALMON . . . 185
GREEK SALAD . . . 24
GREEN CHILI ENCHILADAS . . . 98
GUACAMOLE . . . 6

HAM AND HOMINY . . . 112
HEARTY BEEF SOUP . . . 43
HOT CRAB DIP . . . 12
HOT CRAB HORS D'OEUVRES . . . 13
HOUSE OF REPRESENTATIVES BEAN
    SOUP . . . 40
HOUSTON MEAT AND CHEESE PIE . . . 119
HUNGARIAN RHAPSODY DESSERT . . . 257

ICE BOX PIE . . . 245
INDIAN-STYLE VEGETABLES . . . 69
IRISH SODA BREAD . . . 203
ITALIAN MEAT PIE . . . 118
ITALIAN SPAGHETTI SAUCE . . . 139
ITALIAN ZUCCHINI CASSEROLE . . . 70

JACK'S HOMEMADE CHILI CON
    CARNE . . . 56
JALAPEÑO CORNBREAD . . . 205
JELLO CAKE SUPREME . . . 223
JIM WRIGHT'S CHILI . . . 55
JIM'S FAVORITE OVEN-BARBECUED
    CHICKEN . . . 60

KENTUCKY PIE . . . 244
KEY LIME PIE . . . 251
KIKA'S RIO GRANDE CHILI BEANS . . . 90
KUGELIS (POTATO CASSEROLE) . . . 81

LEFSE (POTATO FLATBREAD) . . . 210
LEMON BARS . . . 230
LEMON CREAM SHERBET . . . 262
LILLIAN'S ROCKY ROAD FUDGE
    BARS . . . 232
LITE AND LEAN BEEF BROIL . . . 128
LOUISIANA SWEET POTATO PIE WITH SOUR
    CREAM TOPPING . . . 246
LYNN'S LASAGNA . . . 115
LYNNE'S CHEESECAKE FOR RUDY . . . 254

MADRAS MEATLOAF . . . 133
MAGGIE CAKE . . . 220
MAINE HADDOCK FILLETS . . . 190
MANDARIN SALAD WITH SWEET AND SOUR
    DRESSING . . . 34
MARGARET CHILES' FRIED CORN . . . 74
MARINATED GREEN BEANS . . . 72
MARINATED VEGETABLE SALAD . . . 20
MARTIN'S DUTCH OVEN MEATLOAF . . . 134
MARY'S BRAN MUFFINS . . . 201
MARY'S SWEET POTATOES WITH CARAMEL
    SAUCE . . . 77
MARY'S TENNESSEE COUNTRY HAM . . . 146
MARYLAND CRAB DIP . . . 11
MARYLAND KIDNEY STEW . . . 64
MEATBALLS POMPA ITALIANO . . . 137
MERAMEC RIVER MUD CHILI . . . 59
MEXICAN CORNBREAD . . . 206
MIKE'S FAVORITE CHICKEN PIE . . . 120
MOBILE-STYLE BAKED CRABS . . . 178
MOTHER DYSON'S MARYLAND STUFFED
    HAM . . . 143
MT. VERNON HAM IN RED WINE . . . 144

NAMELESS CAKE . . . 221
NEW ENGLAND CORN CHOWDER . . . 52
NEW JERSEY BLUEBERRY OR CRANBERRY
    MUFFINS . . . 200

NIPPY CHEESE STRAWS . . . 4

OLD-FASHIONED GEORGIA BRUNSWICK
STEW . . . 62
ORANGE ZUCCHINI BREAD . . . 207
ORANGE-PECAN PIE . . . 243
ORIENTAL CABBAGE SALAD . . . 25
ORIENTAL-STYLE CHICKEN WITH
PEANUTS . . . 162
OVEN-BRAISED WILD DUCK . . . 174
OVERNIGHT LAYERED GREEN SALAD . . . 21
OYSTER STEW (BACHELOR STYLE) . . . 54
OYSTERS À LA OLIVIER . . . 15

P. A.'S BAKED SHRIMP . . . 180
PALACSINTA (HUNGARIAN DESSERT
PANCAKES) . . . 213
PASTA ALLA CHECCA . . . 86
PEACH PIE . . . 250
PEACH SALAD . . . 31
PEAR RELISH . . . 274
PECAN-RITZ PIE . . . 242
PHILIP CRANE'S FAVORITE HAM
LOAF . . . 147
PLUM DUFF . . . 263
POLVORONES . . . 235
POPCORN BALLS . . . 281
PORCUPINES . . . 140
PORK CHOPS AND BROWN RICE
CASSEROLE . . . 110
PORK CHOPS AND SPANISH RICE . . . 108
PORTUGUESE SALAD . . . 32
PRESIDENT REAGAN'S FAVORITE
MACARONI AND CHEESE . . . 94
PRINEVILLE PUMPKIN BREAD . . . 209
PUMPKIN PECAN PIE . . . 240

QUICK AND EASY SCALLOPED
POTATOES . . . 83

RAW CRANBERRY RELISH A LA
NORVEGIENNE . . . 275
RED SPANISH SCAMPI PROVENCALE . . . 181
ROUND STEAK . . . 130

RUDD'S CHILAQUILES . . . 99
RUM CAKE . . . 225

SALMON TARTARE . . . 188
SANDBAKKELSE . . . 261
SANTA FE FIESTA CUCUMBER SOUP . . . 48
SAUSAGE CASSEROLE . . . 114
SAUSAGE SOUFFLÉ . . . 113
SAVORY SEAFOOD CHOWDER . . . 53
SCALLOPED EGGPLANT . . . 71
SEAFOOD MARINARA . . . 184
SEMOLINA CAKE . . . 260
SENATE BEAN SOUP . . . 41
SENATOR BYRD'S FAVORITE CABBAGE
ROLLS . . . 141
SENATOR JOHNSTON'S FAVORITE CHICKEN
SALAD . . . 27
SENATOR'S MIDNIGHT SUPPER . . . 125
SHEPHERD'S PIE . . . 107
SHERRY'S SPAGHETTI SAUCE WITH
MEATBALLS . . . 138
SHRIMP CREOLE . . . 179
SHRIMP FLORENTINE . . . 182
SHRIMP MOUSSE . . . 14
SON-OF-A-BITCH IN A SACK . . . 268
SOUPER EASY, BEEFY RICE
CASSEROLE . . . 84
SOUR CREAM CAKE . . . 222
SOUTH CAROLINA CHICKEN BARBECUE
SAUCE . . . 272
SOUTH DAKOTA TACO SALAD . . . 30
SOY-GINGER CHICKEN . . . 166
SPICY ITALIAN SANDWICHES . . . 124
SPINACH DIP . . . 10
SPLIT PEA SOUP . . . 42
SPOON BREAD . . . 204
SQUASH SOUFFLÉ . . . 76
STUFFED CABBAGE ROLLS . . . 142
SUNDAY BRUNCH CASSEROLE . . . 96
SWEDISH MEATBALLS . . . 136
SWEDISH MEATBALLS . . . 136
SWEDISH PANCAKES . . . 211
SWEDISH RYE BREAD . . . 196
SWEET AND SOUR CHICKEN . . . 164

SWEET AND SOUR PORK . . . 150
SWEET POTATOES IN ORANGE CUPS . . . 78
SWORDFISH EN BROCHETTE . . . 187

TERIYAKI BARBECUED CHICKEN . . . 165
TEX-MEX CHILI AND CHEESE DIP . . . 9
THAD COCHRAN'S FAVORITE MEAT
   LOAF . . . 132

TORTILLA À LA PAISANA . . . 100
TOSSED SALAD . . . 22
TOSTADA GRANDE DIP . . . 5

VEAL SCALLOPINE WITH CHEESE . . . 151
VIRGINIA CRAB IMPERIAL . . . 176

WASHINGTON BARBECUED SALMON . . . 186

ZITI SALAD . . . 29

ABDNOR, SEN. JAMES
DATE-FILLED COOKIES . . . 236
ITALIAN SPAGHETTI SAUCE . . . 139
STUFFED CABBAGE ROLLS . . . 142
ADDABBO, REP. JOSEPH P.
ITALIAN MEAT PIE . . . 118
ANDREWS, SEN. MARK
MARY'S BRAN MUFFINS . . . 201
ANTHONY, REP. BERYL, JR.
OVEN-BRAISED WILD DUCK . . . 174
APPLEGATE, REP. DOUGLAS
MEATBALLS POMPA ITALIANO . . . 137
ARCHER, REP. BILL
CORNBREAD STUFFING . . . 89

BADHAM, REP. ROBERT
SAVORY SEAFOOD CHOWDER . . . 53
BARNES, REP. MICHAEL D.
MARYLAND CRAB DIP . . . 11
BATES, REP. JIM
TERIYAKI BARBECUED CHICKEN . . . 165
BENNETT, REP. CHARLES E.
KEY LIME PIE . . . 251
BENTSEN, SEN. LLOYD
BAKED CRAB IN SHELLS . . . 177
BIDEN, SEN. JOE
CHOCOLATE CREAM CHEESE LAYER CAKE
WITH ICING . . . 218
BILIRAKIS, REP. MICHAEL
GREEK SALAD . . . 24
BLAZ, REP. BEN
ESKABECHI . . . 192
BOEHLERT, REP. SHERWOOD
SHERRY'S SPAGHETTI SAUCE WITH
MEATBALLS . . . 138
BOGGS, REP. LINDY
BAKED GRITS WITH CHEESE . . . 88
CHICKEN TUJAGUE . . . 102
OYSTERS À LA OLIVIER . . . 15
BONKER, REP. DON
AUNT EDA'S NEVER FAIL CHEESE
SOUFFLE . . . 95
BOREN, SEN. DAVID
MAGGIE CAKE . . . 220

BOSCHWITZ, SEN. RUDY
LYNNE'S CHEESECAKE FOR RUDY . . . 254
BOUCHER, REP. RICK
BROWN BREAD . . . 197
BRADLEY, SEN. BILL
NEW JERSEY BLUEBERRY OR CRANBERRY
MUFFINS . . . 200
BROOMFIELD, REP. WILLIAM S.
CHICKEN-BROCCOLI CASSEROLE . . . 103
BROYHILL, SEN. JAMES T.
JIM'S FAVORITE OVEN-BARBECUED
CHICKEN . . . 160
LOUISIANA SWEET POTATO PIE WITH
SOUR CREAM TOPPING . . . 246
BURTON, REP. DAN
CHOCOLATE MELT-AWAY
DESSERT . . . 256
BUSH, VICE PRESIDENT GEORGE
LEMON BARS . . . 230
BYRD, SEN. ROBERT C.
SENATOR BYRD'S FAVORITE CABBAGE
ROLLS . . . 141
BYRON, REP. BEVERLY
BANANA BREAD . . . 208
CHILIES AND CHEESE CASSEROLE . . . 97
COLD CARROT SOUP . . . 47
FRESH TOMATO RELISH . . . 273
PEACH PIE . . . 250
SOY-GINGER CHICKEN . . . 166

CHAFEE, SEN. JOHN H.
SWORDFISH EN BROCHETTE . . . 187
CHANDLER, REP. ROD
HEARTY BEEF SOUP . . . 43
CHAPPELL, REP. BILL
FISH CHOWDER ON-THE-GRILL . . . 191
CHAPPIE, REP. GENE
SEMOLINA CAKE . . . 260
CHENEY, REP. DICK
CHICKEN FLORENTINE . . . 170
CHILES, SEN. LAWTON
MARGARET CHILES' FRIED CORN . . . 74
COBLE, REP. HOWARD
OYSTER STEW (BACHELOR STYLE) . . . 54

COCHRAN, SEN. THAD
    THAD COCHRAN'S FAVORITE MEAT
        LOAF . . . 132
COMBEST, REP. LARRY
    CARAMEL FLAN . . . 266
CONTE, REP. SILVIO
    CHILI CON 'CONTE' . . . 61
COURTER, REP. JIM
    SWEDISH PANCAKES . . . 211
CRAIG, REP. LARRY
    LITE AND LEAN BEEF BROIL . . . 128
CRANE, REP. PHILIP M.
    PHILIP CRANE'S FAVORITE HAM
        LOAF . . . 147
CRANSTON, SEN. ALAN
    SPLIT PEA SOUP . . . 42

DANFORTH, SEN. JOHN
    JACK'S HOMEMADE CHILI CON
        CARNE . . . 56
DARDEN, REP. GEORGE
    LILLIAN'S ROCKY ROAD FUDGE
        BARS . . . 232
DASCHLE, REP. TOM
    SOUTH DAKOTA TACO SALAD . . . 30
DAVIS, REP. ROBERT W.
    COPPER COUNTRY PASTIES . . . 122
de la GARZA, REP. E. (KIKA)
    KIKA'S RIO GRANDE CHILI BEANS . . . 90
    ORANGE-PECAN PIE . . . 243
DE LUGO, REP. RON
    CONCH IN BUTTER SAUCE . . . 183
DeCONCINI, SEN. DENNIS
    NAMELESS CAKE . . . 221
DELAY, REP. TOM
    BIG BEND BEAN DIP . . . 7
    BRAZOS RIVER STEW . . . 63
    GREEN CHILI ENCHILADAS . . . 98
    GUACAMOLE . . . 6
    HOUSTON MEAT AND CHEESE PIE . . . 119
DELLUMS, REP. RON
    DELLUMS' SWEET POTATO PIE . . . 247
DENTON, SEN. JEREMIAH
    MOBILE-STYLE BAKED CRABS . . . 178

DEWINE, REP. MIKE
    MIKE'S FAVORITE CHICKEN PIE . . . 120
DINGELL, REP. JOHN D.
    EASY BUT RICH BEEF CASSEROLE . . . 106
DIXON, SEN. ALAN J.
    AL'S FAVORITE CHILI . . . 57
DOMENICI, SEN. PETE
    SANTA FE FIESTA CUCUMBER SOUP . . . 48
DORGAN, REP. BYRON L.
    CHOCOLATE CHIP PIE . . . 248
DURBIN, REP. RICHARD J.
    KUGELIS (POTATO CASSEROLE) . . . 81
DYSON, REP. ROY
    MOTHER DYSON'S MARYLAND STUFFED
        HAM . . . 143

EAGLETON, SEN. THOMAS F.
    CITRUS LAMB . . . 152
EMERSON, REP. BILL
    BILL'S MISSOURI CHILI . . . 60
EVANS, REP. COOPER
    GRANDMOTHER'S APPLESAUCE
        CAKE . . . 226
EXON, SEN. J. JAMES
    FLOWER POT BREAD . . . 198

FASCELL, REP. DANTE B.
    FETTUCCINE TOSS-UP . . . 85
FEIGHAN, REP. EDWARD F.
    IRISH SODA BREAD . . . 203
FOLEY, REP. THOMAS S.
    HOT CRAB HORS D'OEUVRES . . . 13
FORD, SEN. WENDELL
    KENTUCKY PIE . . . 244
FRANKLIN, REP. WEBB
    ROUND STEAK . . . 130
FROST, REP. MARTIN
    TORTILLA À LA PAISANA . . . 100
FUSTER, REP. JAIME B.
    CHICKEN CROQUETTES . . . 172

GARN, SEN. E. J.
    SWEET AND SOUR PORK . . . 150
GEPHARDT, REP. RICHARD
    BUTTERHORN ROLLS . . . 199

GIBBONS, REP. SAM M.
FRESH STRAWBERRY SALAD . . . 36
GLENN, SEN. JOHN
ANNIE GLENN'S HAM LOAF . . . 148
GLICKMAN, REP. DAN
BROCCOLI OR SPINACH SOUP . . . 45
GONZALEZ, REP. HENRY B.
POLVORONES . . . 235
PORK CHOPS AND SPANISH RICE . . . 108
GORE, SEN. ALBERT, JR.
CHINESE CHICKEN WITH
WALNUTS . . . 161
GORTON, SEN. SLADE
OVERNIGHT LAYERED GREEN
SALAD . . . 21
GUNDERSON, REP. STEVE
LEFSE (POTATO FLATBREAD) . . . 210

HAMILTON, REP. LEE
CREAMED ASPARAGUS . . . 68
SANDBAKKELSE . . . 261
SOUR CREAM CAKE . . . 222
HATCH, SEN. ORRIN G.
FRENCH MINTS . . . 280
HATFIELD, SEN. MARK O.
CHINOOK SALMON CHOWDER . . . 50
CUT A RIBBON CAKE . . . 259
GOOD NEIGHBOR CHICKEN . . . 168
MT. VERNON HAM IN RED WINE . . . 144
SALMON TARTARE . . . 188
HEFLIN, SEN. HOWELL
CHOCOLATE COOKIES . . . 234
HEINZ, SEN. H.J., III
PORTUGUESE SALAD . . . 32
HILLIS, REP. ELWOOD H.
ITALIAN ZUCCHINI CASSEROLE . . . 70
HOLLINGS, SEN. ERNEST F.
CHARLESTON SHE-CRAB SOUP . . . 44
HOLT, REP. MARJORIE S.
DEVILED CRABMEAT CASSEROLE . . . 175
HORTON, REP. FRANK
FRANK AND NANCY'S CAESAR
SALAD . . . 23

HOYER, REP. STENY
BAKED FRUIT . . . 277
HUTTO, REP. EARL
COVE HOTEL PUNCH . . . 278
HYDE, REP. HENRY J.
RED SPANISH SCAMPI
PROVENCALE . . . 181

INOUYE, SEN. DANIEL
FRUIT COCKTAIL CAKE . . . 224
IRELAND, REP. ANDY
CHICKEN-PASTA SALAD . . . 28

JOHNSON, REP. NANCY L.
PLUM DUFF . . . 263
JOHNSTON, SEN. J. BENNETT
SENATOR JOHNSTON'S FAVORITE
CHICKEN SALAD . . . 27
JONES, REP. ED
RUM CAKE . . . 225

KASICH, REP. JOHN
PORCUPINES . . . 140
KASSEBAUM, SEN. NANCY LANDON
ICE BOX PIE . . . 245
KASTEN, SEN. BOB
BRATS 'N KRAUT . . . 149
KEMP, REP. JACK
MEXICAN CORNBREAD . . . 206
KENNEDY, SEN. EDWARD
CAPE COD FISH CHOWDER . . . 51
KENNELLY, REP. BARBARA B.
INDIAN-STYLE VEGETABLES . . . 69
KINDNESS, REP. THOMAS N.
DAVID EYRE PANCAKE . . . 212

LANTOS, REP. TOM
HUNGARIAN RHAPSODY DESSERT . . . 257
LATTA, REP. DELBERT L.
CHICKEN SUPREME . . . 169
LAXALT, SEN. PAUL
JALAPEÑO CORNBREAD . . . 205
LEHMAN, REP. BILL
JALAPENO CORNBREAD . . . 205

LEHMAN, REP. BILL
FRIED OKRA . . . 75
LEVIN, SEN. CARL
CARROT CAKE . . . 228
LIVINGSTON, REP. ROBERT L.
AVOCADO AND SHRIMP IN BUTTER
SAUCE . . . 16
LONG, SEN. RUSSELL B.
SHRIMP CREOLE . . . 179
LOTT, REP. TRENT
P. A.'S BAKED SHRIMP . . . 180
LOWRY, REP. MIKE
WASHINGTON BARBECUED
SALMON . . . 186
LUGAR, SEN. RICHARD G.
SENATOR'S MIDNIGHT SUPPER . . . 125

MACK, REP. CONNIE
SOUPER EASY, BEEFY RICE
CASSEROLE . . . 83
MADIGAN, REP. EDWARD
ORANGE ZUCCHINI BREAD . . . 207
MARTIN, REP. LYNN
LYNN'S LASAGNA . . . 115
MARTIN'S DUTCH OVEN
MEATLOAF . . . 133
MATHIAS, SEN. CHARLES McC., JR.
MARYLAND KIDNEY STEW . . . 63
MATSUNAGA, SEN. SPARK M.
BEEF SUKIYAKI . . . 131
MATTINGLY, SEN. MACK
CRANBERRY FRAPPÉ . . . 276
MAZZOLI, REP. ROMANO L.
BAKED LASAGNA WITH ITALIAN
SAUCE . . . 116
McCURDY, REP. DAVE
AMAZING CHOCOLATE BROWNIES . . . 231
McEWEN, REP. BOB
SAUSAGE CASSEROLE . . . 113
McGRATH, REP. RAY
SEAFOOD MARINARA . . . 183
McHUGH, REP. MATTHEW F.
DARK CHOCOLATE CAKE . . . 219

McKERNAN, REP. JOHN R.
MAINE HADDOCK FILLETS . . . 190
METZENBAUM, SEN. HOWARD M.
GAZPACHO . . . 49
MICA, REP. DANIEL A.
CHINESE SHREDDED CHICKEN
SALAD . . . 26
MICHEL, REP. ROBERT H.
BOURBON SWEET POTATOES . . . 79
MITCHELL, SEN. GEORGE J.
NEW ENGLAND CORN CHOWDER . . . 52
MONTGOMERY, REP. G. V.
SPOON BREAD . . . 203
MORRISON, REP. SID
ORIENTAL CABBAGE SALAD . . . 25
MURKOWSKI, SEN. FRANK
GREAT BARBECUED KENAI
SALMON . . . 185
MYERS, REP. JOHN T.
TOSTADA GRANDE DIP . . . 5

NICKLES, SEN. DON
CROCKPOT CORNISH HENS . . . 173
NUNN, SEN. SAM
GEORGIA PECAN PIE . . . 241

O'NEILL, REP. THOMAS P., JR.
HOUSE OF REPRESENTATIVES BEAN
SOUP . . . 40
OAKAR, REP. MARY ROSE
FROZEN RASPBERRY PIE . . . 252

PACKWOOD, SEN. BOB
SHEPHERD'S PIE . . . 107
TEX-MEX CHILI AND CHEESE DIP . . . 9
PENNY, REP. TIM
COPPER CARROT PENNIES . . . 73
PETRI, REP. THOMAS E.
RAW CRANBERRY RELISH A LA
NORVEGIENNE . . . 275
PICKLE, REP. J. J.
PEAR RELISH . . . 273

QUAYLE, SEN. DAN
CHEESECAKE . . . 253

RAY, REP. RICHARD
FRESH PEACH DAIQUIRI . . . 279
OLD-FASHIONED GEORGIA BRUNSWICK
STEW . . . 62
PECAN-RITZ PIE . . . 242
SWEET POTATOES IN ORANGE
CUPS . . . 78
REAGAN, PRESIDENT RONALD
PRESIDENT REAGAN'S FAVORITE
MACARONI AND CHEESE . . . 93
PUMPKIN PECAN PIE . . . 240
REGULA, REP. RALPH
SCALLOPED EGGPLANT . . . 71
ROBERTS, REP. PAT
HAM AND HOMINY . . . 112
ROBINSON, REP. TOMMY
DUCK AND WILD RICE CASSEROLE . . . 103
ROCKEFELLER, SEN. JAY
SUNDAY BRUNCH CASSEROLE . . . 96
ROSTENKOWSKI, REP. DAN
ORIENTAL-STYLE CHICKEN WITH
PEANUTS . . . 162
ROWLAND, REP. J. ROY
SHRIMP FLORENTINE . . . 182
RUDD, REP. ELDON
CHALUPA CASSEROLE . . . 111
RUDD'S CHILAQUILES . . . 99
RUDMAN, SEN. WARREN
SQUASH SOUFFLÉ . . . 76

SASSER, SEN. JIM
MARY'S SWEET POTATOES WITH
CARAMEL SAUCE . . . 77
MARY'S TENNESSEE COUNTRY
HAM . . . 146
SCHNEIDER, REP. CLAUDINE
APPLE CAKE . . . 227
SCHROEDER, REP. PATRICIA
SHRIMP MOUSSE . . . 13
SCHULZE, REP. RICHARD T.
GERMAN COFFEE CAKE . . . 229

SEIBERLING, REP. JOHN
PORK CHOPS AND BROWN RICE
CASSEROLE . . . 110
SENSENBRENNER, REP. F. JAMES, JR.
CARAMEL BRIE . . . 267
SHARP, REP. PHILIP
ELECTION DAY CHILI . . . 58
SIMON, SEN. PAUL
SAUSAGE SOUFFLÉ . . . 113
SWEET AND SOUR CHICKEN . . . 163
SIMPSON, SEN. ALAN K.
SON-OF-A-BITCH IN A SACK . . . 268
SKELTON, REP. IKE
MARINATED VEGETABLE SALAD . . . 20
SMITH, REP. DENNY
MADRAS MEATLOAF . . . 133
PRINEVILLE PUMPKIN BREAD . . . 209
SMITH, REP. NEAL
BAKING POWDER BISCUITS . . . 202
POPCORN BALLS . . . 281
SMITH, REP. ROBERT C.
JELLO CAKE SUPREME . . . 223
SNOWE, REP. OLYMPIA J.
BAKLAVA . . . 263
STAFFORD, SEN. ROBERT T.
LEMON CREAM SHERBET . . . 262
STALLINGS, REP. RICHARD
QUICK AND EASY SCALLOPED
POTATOES . . . 83
STENHOLM, REP. CHARLES W.
SWEDISH MEATBALLS . . . 136
SWEDISH RYE BREAD . . . 196
STENNIS, SEN. JOHN C.
NIPPY CHEESE STRAWS . . . 3
SWINDALL, REP. PATRICK L.
SPINACH DIP . . . 10
SYMMS, SEN. STEVEN D.
BROWN SUGAR APPLE PIE . . . 249
COMPANY POTATO CASSEROLE . . . 82

TALLON, REP. ROBIN
CHICKEN BOG . . . 158
TAUKE, REP. TOM
CHOCOLATE ANGELFOOD
DESSERT . . . 258

THOMAS, REP. LINDSAY
COUNTRY CAPTAIN CHICKEN . . . 156
THURMOND, SEN. STROM
SOUTH CAROLINA CHICKEN BARBECUE
SAUCE . . . 272
TRAFICANT, REP. JAMES A., JR.
TOSSED SALAD . . . 22
ZITI SALAD . . . 29
TRAXLER, REP. BOB
SENATE BEAN SOUP . . . 41
TRIBLE, SEN. PAUL
HOT CRAB DIP . . . 12
VIRGINIA CRAB IMPERIAL . . . 176

UDALL, REP. MORRIS K.
CHICKEN IN WINE . . . 167

VENTO, REP. BRUCE
SPICY ITALIAN SANDWICHES . . . 123
VOLKMER, REP. HAROLD L.
CORN PUDDING CASSEROLE . . . 80

WEICKER, SEN. LOWELL, JR.
VEAL SCALLOPINE WITH CHEESE . . . 151
WEISS, REP. TED
PALACSINTA (HUNGARIAN DESSERT
PANCAKES) . . . 213

WILLIAMS, REP. PAT
BUTTE PASTY . . . 121
WILSON, SEN. PETE
CALIENTE HOT DIP . . . 8
MARINATED GREEN BEANS . . . 72
WISE, REP. BOB
CHICKEN IN THE POT . . . 159
WRIGHT, REP. JIM
JIM WRIGHT'S CHILI . . . 55
WYLIE, REP. CHALMERS
CHILLED OLIVE-ASPARAGUS SOUP . . . 46
MANDARIN SALAD WITH SWEET AND
SOUR DRESSING . . . 33
PEACH SALAD . . . 31

YOUNG, REP. ROBERT A.
MERAMEC RIVER MUD CHILI . . . 59
ZORINSKY, SEN. ED
BEEF PEPPER STEAK . . . 129
ZSCHAU, REP. ED
PASTA ALLA CHECCA . . . 86

INDEX BY STATE

LEMON BARS . . . 230
PRESIDENT REAGAN'S FAVORITE
   MACARONI AND CHEESE . . . 94
PUMPKIN PECAN PIE . . . 240

ALABAMA
   CHOCOLATE COOKIES . . . 234
   MOBILE-STYLE BAKED CRABS . . . 178

ALASKA
   GREAT BARBECUED KENAI
      SALMON . . . 185

ARIZONA
   CHALUPA CASSEROLE . . . 111
   CHICKEN IN WINE . . . 167
   NAMELESS CAKE . . . 221
   RUDD'S CHILAQUILES . . . 99

ARKANSAS
   DUCK AND WILD RICE
      CASSEROLE . . . 104
   OVEN-BRAISED WILD DUCK . . . 174

CALIFORNIA
   CALIENTE HOT DIP . . . 8
   DELLUMS' SWEET POTATO PIE . . . 247
   HUNGARIAN RHAPSODY DESSERT . . . 257
   MARINATED GREEN BEANS . . . 72
   PASTA ALLA CHECCA . . . 86
   SAVORY SEAFOOD CHOWDER . . . 53
   SEMOLINA CAKE . . . 260
   SPLIT PEA SOUP . . . 42
   TERIYAKI BARBECUED CHICKEN . . . 165

COLORADO
   SHRIMP MOUSSE . . . 14

CONNECTICUT
   INDIAN-STYLE VEGETABLES . . . 69
   PLUM DUFF . . . 263
   VEAL SCALLOPINE WITH CHEESE . . . 151

DELAWARE
   CHOCOLATE CREAM CHEESE LAYER
      CAKE WITH ICING . . . 218

FLORIDA
   CHICKEN-PASTA SALAD . . . 28
   CHINESE SHREDDED CHICKEN
      SALAD . . . 26
   COVE HOTEL PUNCH . . . 278
   FETTUCCINE TOSS-UP . . . 85
   FISH CHOWDER ON-THE-GRILL . . . 191
   FRESH STRAWBERRY SALAD . . . 36
   FRIED OKRA . . . 75
   GREEK SALAD . . . 24
   KEY LIME PIE . . . 251
   MARGARET CHILES' FRIED CORN . . . 74
   SOUPER EASY, BEEFY RICE
      CASSEROLE . . . 84

GEORGIA
   COUNTRY CAPTAIN CHICKEN . . . 156
   CRANBERRY FRAPPÉ . . . 276
   FRESH PEACH DAIQUIRI . . . 279
   GEORGIA PECAN PIE . . . 241
   LILLIAN'S ROCKY ROAD FUDGE
      BARS . . . 232
   OLD-FASHIONED GEORGIA BRUNSWICK
      STEW . . . 62
   PECAN-RITZ PIE . . . 242
   SHRIMP FLORENTINE . . . 182
   SPINACH DIP . . . 10
   SWEET POTATOES IN ORANGE
      CUPS . . . 78

GUAM
   ESKABECHI . . . 192

HAWAII
   BEEF SUKIYAKI . . . 131
   FRUIT COCKTAIL CAKE . . . 224

IDAHO
   BROWN SUGAR APPLE PIE . . . 249
   COMPANY POTATO CASSEROLE . . . 82

LITE AND LEAN BEEF BROIL . . . 128
QUICK AND EASY SCALLOPED
   POTATOES . . . 83

ILLINOIS
AL'S FAVORITE CHILI . . . 57
BOURBON SWEET POTATOES . . . 79
KUGELIS (POTATO CASSEROLE) . . . 81
LYNN'S LASAGNA . . . 115
MARTIN'S DUTCH OVEN MEATLOAF134
ORANGE ZUCCHINI BREAD . . . 207
ORIENTAL-STYLE CHICKEN WITH
   PEANUTS . . . 162
PHILIP CRANE'S FAVORITE HAM
   LOAF . . . 147
RED SPANISH SCAMPI
   PROVENCALE . . . 181
SAUSAGE SOUFFLÉ . . . 113
SWEET AND SOUR CHICKEN . . . 164

INDIANA
CHEESECAKE . . . 253
CHOCOLATE MELT-AWAY
   DESSERT . . . 256
CREAMED ASPARAGUS . . . 68
ELECTION DAY CHILI . . . 58
ITALIAN ZUCCHINI CASSEROLE . . . 70
SANDBAKKELSE . . . 261
SENATOR'S MIDNIGHT SUPPER . . . 125
SOUR CREAM CAKE . . . 222
TOSTADA GRANDE DIP . . . 5

IOWA
BAKING POWDER BISCUITS . . . 202
CHOCOLATE ANGELFOOD
   DESSERT . . . 258
GRANDMOTHER'S APPLESAUCE
   CAKE . . . 226
POPCORN BALLS . . . 281

KANSAS
BROCCOLI OR SPINACH SOUP . . . 45
HAM AND HOMINY . . . 112
ICE BOX PIE . . . 245

KENTUCKY
BAKED LASAGNA WITH ITALIAN
   SAUCE . . . 116
KENTUCKY PIE . . . 244

LOUISIANA
AVOCADO AND SHRIMP IN BUTTER
   SAUCE . . . 16
BAKED GRITS WITH CHEESE . . . 88
CHICKEN TUJAGUE . . . 102
OYSTERS À LA OLIVIER . . . 15
SENATOR JOHNSTON'S FAVORITE
   CHICKEN SALAD . . . 27
SHRIMP CREOLE . . . 179

MAINE
BAKLAVA . . . 264
MAINE HADDOCK FILLETS . . . 190
NEW ENGLAND CORN CHOWDER . . . 52

MARYLAND
BAKED FRUIT . . . 277
BANANA BREAD . . . 208
CHILIES AND CHEESE CASSEROLE . . . 97
COLD CARROT SOUP . . . 47
DEVILED CRABMEAT CASSEROLE . . . 175
FRESH TOMATO RELISH . . . 273
MARYLAND CRAB DIP . . . 11
MARYLAND KIDNEY STEW . . . 64
MOTHER DYSON'S MARYLAND STUFFED
   HAM . . . 143
PEACH PIE . . . 250
SOY-GINGER CHICKEN . . . 166

MASSACHUSETTS
CAPE COD FISH CHOWDER . . . 51
CHILI CON 'CONTE' . . . 61
HOUSE OF REPRESENTATIVES BEAN
   SOUP . . . 40

MICHIGAN
CARROT CAKE . . . 228
CHICKEN-BROCCOLI CASSEROLE . . . 103
COPPER COUNTRY PASTIES . . . 122

Index by State

EASY BUT RICH BEEF CASSEROLE . . . 106
SENATE BEAN SOUP . . . 41

MINNESOTA
COPPER CARROT PENNIES . . . 73
LYNNE'S CHEESECAKE FOR RUDY . . . 254
SPICY ITALIAN SANDWICHES . . . 124

MISSISSIPPI
NIPPY CHEESE STRAWS . . . 4
P. A.'S BAKED SHRIMP . . . 180
ROUND STEAK . . . 130
SPOON BREAD . . . 204
THAD COCHRAN'S FAVORITE MEAT
LOAF . . . 132

MISSOURI
BILL'S MISSOURI CHILI . . . 60
BUTTERHORN ROLLS . . . 199
CITRUS LAMB . . . 152
CORN PUDDING CASSEROLE . . . 80
JACK'S HOMEMADE CHILI CON
CARNE . . . 56
MARINATED VEGETABLE SALAD . . . 20
MERAMEC RIVER MUD CHILI . . . 59

MONTANA
BUTTE PASTY . . . 121

NEBRASKA
BEEF PEPPER STEAK . . . 129
FLOWER POT BREAD . . . 198

NEVADA
JALAPEÑO CORNBREAD . . . 205

NEW HAMPSHIRE
JELLO CAKE SUPREME . . . 223
SQUASH SOUFFLÉ . . . 76

NEW JERSEY
NEW JERSEY BLUEBERRY OR CRANBERRY
MUFFINS . . . 200
SWEDISH PANCAKES . . . 211

NEW MEXICO
SANTA FE FIESTA CUCUMBER
SOUP . . . 48

NEW YORK
ARK CHOCOLATE CAKE . . . 219
FRANK AND NANCY'S CAESAR
SALAD . . . 23
ITALIAN MEAT PIE . . . 118
MEXICAN CORNBREAD . . . 206
PALACSINTA (HUNGARIAN DESSERT
PANCAKES) . . . 213
SEAFOOD MARINARA . . . 184
SHERRY'S SPAGHETTI SAUCE WITH
MEATBALLS . . . 138

NORTH CAROLINA
JIM'S FAVORITE OVEN-BARBECUED
CHICKEN . . . 160
LOUISIANA SWEET POTATO PIE WITH
SOUR CREAM TOPPING . . . 246
OYSTER STEW (BACHELOR STYLE) . . . 54

NORTH DAKOTA
CHOCOLATE CHIP PIE . . . 248
MARY'S BRAN MUFFINS . . . 201

OHIO
ANNIE GLENN'S HAM LOAF . . . 148
CHICKEN SUPREME . . . 169
CHILLED OLIVE-ASPARAGUS SOUP . . . 46
DAVID EYRE PANCAKE . . . 212
FROZEN RASPBERRY PIE . . . 252
GAZPACHO . . . 49
IRISH SODA BREAD . . . 203
MANDARIN SALAD WITH SWEET AND
SOUR DRESSING . . . 34
MEATBALLS POMPA ITALIANO . . . 137
MIKE'S FAVORITE CHICKEN PIE . . . 120
PEACH SALAD . . . 31
PORCUPINES . . . 140
PORK CHOPS AND BROWN RICE
CASSEROLE . . . 110
SAUSAGE CASSEROLE . . . 114

SCALLOPED EGGPLANT . . . 71
TOSSED SALAD . . . 22
ZITI SALAD . . . 29

OKLAHOMA
AMAZING CHOCOLATE
BROWNIES . . . 231
CROCKPOT CORNISH HENS . . . 173
MAGGIE CAKE . . . 220

OREGON
CHINOOK SALMON CHOWDER . . . 50
CUT A RIBBON CAKE . . . 259
GOOD NEIGHBOR CHICKEN . . . 168
MADRAS MEATLOAF . . . 133
MT. VERNON HAM IN RED WINE . . . 144
PRINEVILLE PUMPKIN BREAD . . . 209
SALMON TARTARE . . . 188
SHEPHERD'S PIE . . . 107
TEX-MEX CHILI AND CHEESE DIP . . . 9

PENNSYLVANIA
GERMAN COFFEE CAKE . . . 229
PORTUGUESE SALAD . . . 32

PUERTO RICO
CHICKEN CROQUETTES . . . 172

RHODE ISLAND
APPLE CAKE . . . 227
SWORDFISH EN BROCHETTE . . . 187

SOUTH CAROLINA
CHARLESTON SHE-CRAB SOUP . . . 44
CHICKEN BOG . . . 158
SOUTH CAROLINA CHICKEN BARBECUE
SAUCE . . . 272

SOUTH DAKOTA
DATE-FILLED COOKIES . . . 236
ITALIAN SPAGHETTI SAUCE . . . 139
SOUTH DAKOTA TACO SALAD . . . 30
STUFFED CABBAGE ROLLS . . . 142

TENNESSEE
CHINESE CHICKEN WITH
WALNUTS . . . 161
MARY'S SWEET POTATOES WITH
CARAMEL SAUCE . . . 77
MARY'S TENNESSEE COUNTRY
HAM . . . 146
RUM CAKE . . . 225

TEXAS
BAKED CRAB IN SHELLS . . . 177
BIG BEND BEAN DIP . . . 7
BRAZOS RIVER STEW . . . 63
CARAMEL FLAN . . . 266
CORNBREAD STUFFING . . . 89
GREEN CHILI ENCHILADAS . . . 98
GUACAMOLE . . . 6
HOUSTON MEAT AND CHEESE PIE . . . 119
JIM WRIGHT'S CHILI . . . 55
KIKA'S RIO GRANDE CHILI BEANS . . . 90
ORANGE-PECAN PIE . . . 243
PEAR RELISH . . . 274
POLVORONES . . . 235
PORK CHOPS AND SPANISH RICE . . . 108
SWEDISH MEATBALLS . . . 136
SWEDISH RYE BREAD . . . 196
TORTILLA À LA PAISANA . . . 100

UTAH
FRENCH MINTS . . . 280
SWEET AND SOUR PORK . . . 150

VERMONT
LEMON CREAM SHERBET . . . 262
VIRGIN ISLANDS . . . CONCH IN BUTTER
SAUCE . . . 183

VIRGINIA
BROWN BREAD . . . 197
HOT CRAB DIP . . . 12
VIRGINIA CRAB IMPERIAL . . . 176

WASHINGTON
AUNT EDA'S NEVER FAIL CHEESE
SOUFFLE . . . 95
HEARTY BEEF SOUP . . . 43
HOT CRAB HORS D'OEUVRES . . . 13
ORIENTAL CABBAGE SALAD . . . 25
OVERNIGHT LAYERED GREEN
SALAD . . . 21
WASHINGTON BARBECUED
SALMON . . . 186

WEST VIRGINIA
CHICKEN IN THE POT . . . 159
SENATOR BYRD'S FAVORITE CABBAGE
ROLLS . . . 141
SUNDAY BRUNCH CASSEROLE . . . 96

WISCONSIN
BRATS 'N KRAUT . . . 149
CARAMEL BRIE . . . 267
LEFSE (POTATO FLATBREAD) . . . 210
RAW CRANBERRY RELISH A LA
NORVEGIENNE . . . 275

WYOMING
CHICKEN FLORENTINE . . . 170
SON-OF-A-BITCH IN A SACK . . . 268